HAROLD
PINTER

WORLD DRAMATISTS

HAROLD
PINTER

RONALD HAYMAN

WITH HALFTONE ILLUSTRATIONS

FREDERICK UNGAR PUBLISHING CO.
NEW YORK

First American publication 1973

© 1968, 1969, 1973 by Ronald Hayman
Printed in the United States of America
Library of Congress Catalog Card Number: 72-79936
Designed by Edith Fowler
ISBN 0-8044-2371-7 (cloth)

ACKNOWLEDGMENTS

The Author would like to thank Catherine Barton, Martha Crewe, John Peter, Charles Tomlinson and Irving Wardle for their help in reading typescripts and making useful comments, when the series was in preparation.

The Author and Publishers wish to thank the following for permission to include quotations from the publications listed below:

Johnson over Jordan: J. B. Priestley and A. D. Peters & Co; *The Homecoming, The Collection, The Lover, Night School, A Slight Ache, The Room, The Dumb Waiter, The Birthday Party, A Night Out, The Caretaker, The Basement, Last to Go, The Dwarfs, Tea Party, Landscape, Silence, Night,* and *Old Times*: Harold Pinter and Methuen & Co Ltd.

CONTENTS

CHRONOLOGY

1930   Born in Hackney, the only child of an East End Jewish tailor.

1948   Started an interrupted training at the Royal Academy of Dramatic Art. Refused to do National Service. On trial twice as a conscientious objector.

1949   Wrote first fragment of dramatic dialogue, *Kullus*.

1950   Two poems published in *Poetry London*, August. First job as an actor—in a radio feature, *Focus on Football Pools*, September.

1951   Resumed training at Central School of Speech and Drama.

1951–52   Toured Ireland in Anew McMaster's company.

1953   Acted in Donald Wolfit's season at King's Theatre, Hammersmith. Met Vivien Merchant.

1954–57   Adopted stage name of David Barron. Worked in various provincial repertory companies. When out of work he took jobs as a waiter, a doorman, a dishwasher and a door-to-door salesman.

1956   Met Vivien Merchant again while at the Palace Court Theatre, Bournemouth. They were married that year.

1957   Wrote *The Room* during four afternoons while in weekly repertory at Devon, rehearsing in the mornings and playing in the evenings. Henry Woolf, who was studying at the Drama Department of Bristol University and had asked for the play, directed it there. After seeing the production Pinter went on to write *The Dumb Waiter* and *The Birthday Party*. *The Room* was also produced by students of the Bristol Old Vic at a student drama competition sponsored by the *Sunday Times*. Harold Hobson, its drama critic, was one of the judges.

1958   On reading what Hobson wrote about the play, Michael Codron, an independent producer, asked to see some other things by Pinter. Birth of Pinter's son, Daniel.

Codron bought an option on *The Birthday Party* for £50. After one unperformed radio play, *Something in Common*, he wrote *A Slight Ache*, which was commissioned by the BBC.

1959   Wrote *A Night Out* and *The Caretaker*. Contributed two sketches "Trouble in the Works" and "The Black and the White" to the *New Lyric Revue*, presented by Codron at Hammersmith in July.

1960   Wrote *Night School* and the radio version of *The Dwarfs* based on an earlier autobiographical novel.

Took over the part of Mick in the West End

production of *The Caretaker* for four weeks
from 21 February.

1961   Wrote *The Collection.*

1962   Wrote *The Lover* and screenplays for *The
Caretaker* and *The Servant* (based on Robin
Maugham's short novel). Co-directed the
Royal Shakespeare Company's production
of *The Collection*, with Peter Hall.

1963   Wrote the screenplay for *The Pumpkin
Eater* (based on Penelope Mortimer's
novel).

1964   Wrote *Tea Party* and *The Homecoming.*
Directed *The Birthday Party* for the Royal
Shakespeare Company.

1965   Played in Philip Saville's television produc-
tion of Sartre's *Huis Clos* (*No Exit*), with
Jane Arden and Katherine Woodville.
Wrote screenplay for *The Quiller Memo-
randum* (from Jonquil Trevor's novel *The
Berlin Memorandum*).

1966   Awarded a C.B.E. (Commander of the Or-
der of the British Empire).
Wrote screenplay for *Accident* (based on
Nicholas Mosley's novel) and played in it.

1967   Played Stott in television production of *The
Basement.* Directed Robert Shaw's play *The
Man in the Glass Booth*, with Donald
Pleasence.

1968   Wrote *Landscape* and the screenplay of
The Birthday Party.

1969   Wrote *Silence* and the screenplay of *The
Go-Between*, based on L. P. Hartley's novel.

1970   Wrote *Old Times* and directed James
Joyce's *Exiles.*

1971   Directed Simon Gray's *Butley.*

1973   Appointed by Peter Hall as an Associate
Director of the National Theatre.

HAROLD PINTER

No adjectives have been derived from the names of Osborne, Beckett, Whiting, Miller or Albee, but the word "Pinteresque" is already familiar, which must mean that his style is the most distinctive, or at least the most easily recognizable.

Pinter has capitalized in a way that no playwright had ever done before—though many have since—on the fact that real-life conversations don't proceed smoothly and logically from point to point. Conventional characters in conventional plays listen to each other intently and answer each other intelligently, but few people do this in reality. Nonrealistic plays like *Waiting for Godot* (1953) and Ionesco's *The Bald Soprano* (1948) used nonlogical sequences in the dialogue, and in this respect at least they were realistic in reflecting the way human consciousness works. But Pinter was doing something new by making realistic characters in realistic settings talk as repetitiously and inconsequentially as people in fact do talk. He has an accurate and affectionate ear for the irrationality of dialogue, and not only working-class dialogue, though it's the working-class characters who make it stand out in the clearest relief, as in the revue sketch *Last to Go*.

> MAN: I went to see if I could get hold of George.
> BARMAN: Who?
> MAN: George.
> *(Pause.)*
> BARMAN: George who?
> MAN: George . . . whatsisname.
> BARMAN: Oh.
> *(Pause.)*
> Did you get hold of him?
> MAN: No. No, I couldn't get hold of him. I couldn't locate him.
> BARMAN: He's not about much now, is he?
> *(Pause.)*
> MAN: When did you last see him then?
> BARMAN: Oh, I haven't seen him for years.
> MAN: No, nor me.
> *(Pause.)*
> BARMAN: Used to suffer very bad from arthritis.
> MAN: Arthritis?
> BARMAN: Yes.
> MAN: He never suffered from arthritis.
> BARMAN: Suffered very bad.
> *(Pause.)*
> MAN: Not when I knew him.
> *(Pause.)*
> BARMAN: I think he must have left the area.
> *(Pause.)*
> MAN: Yes, it was the *Evening News* was the last to go tonight.

BARMAN: Not always the last though, is it, though?

MAN: No. Oh no. I mean sometimes it's the *News*. Other times it's one of the others. No way of telling beforehand. Until you've got your last one left, of course. Then you can tell which one it's going to be.

BARMAN: Yes.

(Pause.)

MAN: Oh yes.

(Pause.)

I think he must have left the area.

This is writing which succeeds by breaking all the rules of writing. It's good because it's so realistically full of bad syntax, tautologies, pleonasms, repetitions, *non sequiturs* and self-contradictions. The characters are not only uninterested in listening, they are hardly interested in what they themselves are saying.

This passage is a fair example of what would be regarded as Pinteresque. But in a sense it's unfortunate for a writer when an adjective like this becomes so very common so very soon. It's also misleading, because it suggests that what's typical of him at one stage of his development is also typical of every other, that his style has remained at a standstill.

Pinter's hasn't. We see him using the same tricks of circling repetitious and tangential irrelevancies in the plays, not always to such great comic effect, but more subtly. For example, in *The Caretaker*:

DAVIES: I can't move without them papers. They tell you who I am. You see! I'm stuck without them.

ASTON: Why's that?

> DAVIES: You see, what it is, you see, I changed
> my name! Years ago. I been going around un-
> der an assumed name! That's not my real
> name.
>
> ASTON: What name you been going under?
>
> DAVIES: Jenkins. Bernard Jenkins. That's my
> name. That's the name I'm known, anyway.
> But it's no good me going on with that name. I
> got no rights. I got an insurance card here.
> (*He takes a card from his pocket.*) Under the
> name of Jenkins. See? Bernard Jenkins. Look.
> It's got four stamps on it. Four of them. But I
> can't go along with these.

Here, Davies's character is shaped largely through
the jumping of his grasshopper mind from one subject to the other, always evading the real point. The
rhythm of procrastination can be heard in every sentence he utters. The language has become a function
of the character just as the character is a function of
the theme. The evasion of points, in action as in
speech, is the main subject of the play.

Pinter's earlier plays are closer to the revue sketch
in style. The repetitiveness, the inconsequentiality,
and the irrationality are served up as objects of interest in themselves. For example, in *The Room*:

> MR. KIDD: . . . She's been dead some time now,
> my sister. It was a good house then. She was a
> capable woman. Yes. Fine size of a woman too.
> I think she took after my mum. Yes, I think
> she took after my old mum, from what I can
> recollect. I think my mum was a Jewess. Yes, I
> wouldn't be surprised to learn that she was a
> Jewess. She didn't have many babies.
>
> ROSE: What about your sister, Mr. Kidd?

Mr. Kidd: What about her?

Rose Did she have any babies?

Mr. Kidd: Yes, she had a resemblance to my old mum, I think. Taller, of course.

Rose: When did she die then, your sister?

Mr. Kidd: Yes, that's right, it was after she died that I must have stopped counting. She used to keep things in very good trim.

Here he is already exploring new areas of verbal comedy, but later, as the technique is refined, there is a more subtly humorous enjoyment in the weird progressions of the characters' thoughts. The *non sequiturs* in Meg's speech at Stanley's birthday party show up the ghastliness of her sentimentality with searchlight clarity, which is both remorseless and affectionate.

Well—it's very, very nice to be here tonight, in my house, and I want to propose a toast to Stanley, because it's his birthday, and he's lived here for a long while now, and he's my Stanley now. And I think he's a good boy, although sometimes he's bad. (*An appreciative laugh from Goldberg.*) And he's the only Stanley I know, and I know him better than all the world, although he doesn't think so. (*"Hear—hear" from Goldberg.*) Well, I could cry because I'm so happy, having him here and not gone away, on his birthday, and there isn't anything I wouldn't do for him, and all you good people here tonight . . . (*She sobs.*)

And in *The Collection*, the technique is still further developed with a new and acid precision in the tersely economic interlocution. Each repetition and variation has its point.

HARRY: What a beautiful lamp.

STELLA: What can I do for you?

HARRY: Do you know Bill Lloyd?

STELLA: No.

HARRY: Oh, you don't?

STELLA: No.

HARRY: You don't know him personally?

STELLA: I don't, no.

HARRY: I found him in a slum, you know, by accident. Just happened to be in a slum one day and there he was. I realized he had talent straight away. I gave him a roof, gave him a job, and he came up trumps. We've been close friends for years.

STELLA: Oh yes?

HARRY: You know of him, of course, don't you, by repute? He's a dress designer.

STELLA: I know of him.

HARRY: You're both dress designers.

STELLA: Yes.

HARRY: You don't belong to the Rags and Bags Club, do you?

STELLA: The what?

HARRY: The Rags and Bags Club. I thought I might have seen you down there.

STELLA: No, I don't know it.

HARRY: Shame. You'd like it.

(Pause.)

Yes.

(Pause.)

I've come about your husband.

Here the inconsequentiality is harnessed not only to the characterization, as it was with Davies and with Meg, but also to the elaboration of the situation. Harry is tense because he is suspicious of Bill's relationship with Stella and he is revenging himself on her by deliberately confusing her. The inconsequentiality has become a sadistic weapon in the hands of a character who knows what he's doing with it.

One point that Pinter has in common with Osborne is that they both specialize in one-sided dialogues. But they do so in very different ways. The on-stage listeners during Jimmy Porter's monologues (or Archie Rice's or Luther's) are very unimportant. In Pinter the unbalance in the number of words spoken is often just as great. Time and again we get a nagging mother figure like Meg or Rose in *The Room* or the woman in *A Night Out* doing practically all the talking while the husband or son or lodger preserves a protracted silence. But Pinter is far from identifying with the speaker. His focus is always on the fact of unbalance. He's just as interested in the listener— even if he isn't listening—as in the speaker. He seems to have no difficulty in achieving this detachment: it seems natural for him to stand very much farther back from his subject than Osborne does. In *The Homecoming*, when Ruth asks Teddy whether the family has read his "critical works," his answer goes a long way towards defining Pinter's own position— that of standing outside the event as an observer.

> You wouldn't understand my works. You wouldn't have the faintest idea of what they were about. You wouldn't appreciate the points of reference. You're way behind. All of you. There's no point in my sending you my works. You'd be lost. It's nothing to do with the question of intelligence. It's a way of being able to look at the world. It's a question of how far you can operate on things and not in things. I mean it's a question of your

capacity to ally the two, to relate the two, to balance the two. To see, to be able to *see!* I'm the one who can see. That's why I can write my critical works. Might do you good . . . have a look at them . . . see how certain people can view . . . things . . . how certain people can maintain . . . intellectual equilibrium. Intellectual equilibrium. You're just objects. You just . . . move about. I can observe it. I can see what you do. It's the same as I do. But you're lost in it. You won't get me being . . . I won't be lost in it.

No doubt the detachment is an indispensable prerequisite for the accuracy with which Pinter hears and records dialogue. Osborne is a writer who readily commits himself, and not only on political issues. He writes like a good talker and a bad listener. Pinter, who is very loth to commit himself, writes like a compulsive listener, as for example in *Night School*:

BARBARA: What did he say then?

SALLY: Come over with me one Sunday, he says, come over and have Sunday dinner, meet the wife. Why, I said, what are you going to introduce me as, your sister? No, he says, she's very broadminded, my wife, she'll be delighted to meet you.

MAVIS: Oh yes, I've heard of that kind of thing before.

SALLY: Yes, that's what I said. Oh yes, I said, I've heard of that kind of thing before. Go on, get off out of it, I said, buzz off before I call a copper.

BARBARA: Which was he, the one with the big nose?

SALLY: Yes.

The night-club hostesses don't interest Pinter particularly, but he still shows a delight in getting the words and the rhythms right. He's equally effective in completely differing social contexts, but his favorite locales are all-night coffee stalls, transport cafes and milk bars. The excerpt below is from a revue sketch called "The Black and the White."

> SECOND OLD WOMAN: Did you see that one come up and speak to me at the counter?
> FIRST: Who?
> SECOND: Comes up to me, he says, hullo, he says, what's the time by your clock? Bloody liberty. I was just standing there getting your soup.
> FIRST: It's tomato soup.
> SECOND: What's the time by your clock? he says.
> FIRST: I bet you answered him back.
> SECOND: I told him all right. Go on, I said, why don't you get back into your scraghole, I said, clear off out of it before I call a copper.

But he's also master of Edward's idiom in *A Slight Ache*.

> You must excuse my chatting away like this. We have few visitors this time of the year. All our friends summer abroad. I'm a home bird myself. Wouldn't mind taking a trip to Asia Minor, mind you, or to certain lower regions of the Congo, but Europe? Out of the question. Much too noisy. I'm sure you agree.

In developing a style which is as flexible as this, realistic and yet stylized, and capable of covering such a wide social and emotional range, Pinter's achievement has been enormous. But his limitations are also enormous, stemming partly from the detachment. He isn't interested in exploring experience. Basically his vision of the world remains a child's-eye view. He's obsessed with the subject of the safety of the womb or room and the dangers of dispossession.

Many of the men in his work are either dispossessors or dispossessed, and almost all the women are either possessive mother figures or tarts—and so almost impossible to possess. Some are both. Not one is sympathetic. Most are garrulous. Rose, in *The Room*, talks incessantly. There are no women in *The Dumb Waiter*, and in *The Birthday Party* there are Meg, who chatters nonstop to her husband and makes her lodger into a substitute son-cum-lover, and Lulu, who isn't a tart but may end up as one. In *A Slight Ache*, the wife finally gives herself to the matchseller and presents her husband with the old man's match-tray. In *A Night Out* we have the nagging mother and the flirty office girls, who lead Albert on. There are no women in *The Caretaker* and in *Night School* the nagging mother role is divided between the two aunts and a schoolteacher who turns out to be a night-club hostess. *The Dwarfs* has no women in it; the woman in *The Collection* is a brittle enigma; the woman in *The Lover* has to play at being unfaithful, though actually she isn't; the two main women in *Tea Party* are both enigmatic and unsympathetic; and in *The Homecoming* the ex-tart is quite willing to go back to being a tart again.

It's certainly an extraordinary series of parts that Pinter has written for women. It is interesting that when a woman interviewer told him that she found none of his characters likable, the women especially being "extremely feminine in a rather cruel and taunting way," his reply was that he liked them all very much himself and that the women weren't all wicked or all awful from his point of view. But in his determination to "operate on things and not in things" he seems to rein himself back from involvement in his characters' experience, and the women come off far worse than the men.

Not that the men get much sympathy. Davies and Aston come off best. Though acutely aware of everything that stops them from functioning properly, Pinter identifies with them considerably, and they both emerge quite strongly in three dimensions—Davies more than Aston.

But Pinter's whole method of characterization differs sharply from the conventional method we're used to, and which derives from Ibsen. For Ibsen, the past histories of the characters are the soil in which the whole plot is planted. For Pinter, the past histories of the characters, like their off-stage lives and their social backgrounds, couldn't matter less. The only facts that he's concerned with are the facts of what is said and done on stage. In *The Birthday Party*, we only know Stanley's past as he describes it. But there is no interest in getting at the truth behind his falsifications. What's important is that he is falsifying. The focus is always on the here-and-now.

This does not prevent the characters or the social settings from creating a very definite impression. The cheap seaside boarding house of *The Birthday Party* and the room full of accumulated junk in *The Caretaker* strike us as very real, and Goldberg and Meg are both solid characters, though Pinter doesn't tell us much about them. Neither of them is really more than the incarnation of a line of talk. They both "do" things, but their actions don't help much to define them. In fact the extent to which they succeed as "characters" shows how little characters need to be defined. None of Pinter's characters are defined by their past history (which they're liable to distort), their position in society (which they're liable to misrepresent), their attitudes (which are inconsistent), or by their physical appearance (which is seldom described). Generally, we know nothing about them, except what we see and hear for ourselves, and their statements are often self-contradictory, their actions inconsistent.

In withholding from his audiences the clear lines of definition that he knows they crave for, Pinter is pursuing a deliberate policy, as he explains in the program notes for the 1960 production of *The Room* and *The Dumb Waiter*.

> The desire for verification is understandable, but cannot always be satisfied. There are no hard distinctions between what is real and what is unreal, nor between what is true and what false. The thing is not necessarily either true or false; it can be both true and false. The assumption that to verify what has happened and what is happening presents no problems, I take to be inaccurate. A character on the stage who can present no convincing argument or information as to his past experiences, his present behaviour or his aspirations, nor give a comprehensive analysis of his motives is as legitimate and as worthy of attention as one who, alarmingly, can do all these things. The more acute the experience the less articulate its expression.

Pinter's story line is usually subject to the same indefiniteness as his characters. We are often in doubt about whether or not an event has really taken place, because we're never sure whether to believe the characters. Before Pinter and before the other writers in what Martin Esslin has dubbed the Theatre of the Absurd, we could always take it for granted that what a character said on stage was true, unless we were given specific reasons for distrusting him. Pinter cuts right through this convention. In his first play, *The Room*, Mr. Kidd is made to prattle on at great length about his sister but as soon as he goes out of the room, Rose says, "I don't believe he had a sister, ever."

Most drama is built up out of addition. Points are planted one by one until they add up to a plot. Pinter's method often works by subtraction. He plants a point only to uproot it, without ever going into the character's motivations for misrepresenting the reality. So the impossibility of verifying reality becomes not only a source of suspense but also one of the fundamental subjects of his plays.

The plays are thrillers, full of mysteries that are put in with no intention of solving them and no pretence that the playwright himself is in a position to. They work on the audience by spreading out the mystification, enjoying it, and exploring it for its own sake—but never resolving it. Hints are dropped deliberately as if they were clues in the mystery, but the trail of evidence never leads to a solution. Until *The Collection*, the element of mystification is kept fairly well under control, used as a valid ingredient in the play. After *The Lover*, however, what had been a means becomes an end, and the quality of the work suffers. Sometimes, as in *Tea Party*, Pinter's most obscure television play, he uses it in a rather unfair way to titillate the audience's appetite without ever satisfying it. But in the earlier, more controlled plays, the element of mystification is used with more justification.

The Room is full of mysteries. In *The Dumb Waiter* we never find out much about the setup that organizes the murders or why Gus has to be killed. *The Birthday Party* never explains what is behind the take-over bid Goldberg and McCann make for possession of Stanley. In *A Slight Ache*, the motivations of the matchseller are a mystery which torments Edward, who cannot understand why he should stand there day after day, where nobody ever passes, never selling a single box. But for us, the focus is not on the mystery of the old man but on why Edward and Flora react to him in the way they do, as if he were a threat to them. In *The Caretaker*, Mick's teasing enjoyment of violence as a kind of practical joke builds up a great deal of effective stage terror. However, his motivations remain nearly as obscure as those of Goldberg and McCann, who may be under orders, as they say they are; in neither case do we get an explanation. Motives aren't important either for Pinter or for us. In *The Collection*, the whole play hinges on a mystery—what happened in Leeds when Bill and Stella stayed in the same hotel? Did they sleep together or just kiss in the corridor or just sit in the lounge and talk? As the play shows, it doesn't really matter what has happened. What matters is what happens out of it, in the here-and-now. Once an action is in the past tense, there's no way of distinguishing fact from fiction. The two mix together, like hot and cold water in a bath.

PLAYS

The Room

The Room was written early in 1957 and first staged by the Drama Department of Bristol University, but it wasn't given a professional production until the Hampstead Theatre Club put it on in January 1960.

It gives a first airing to many of the preoccupations which have since become familiar from Pinter's other plays. Rose isn't a mother, but she's the prototype of all Pinter's chattering, fussing, nagging mother-figures; women never stop to listen, but they also never stop asking implicitly for the goodwill of the husband or son or nephew or lodger. The play opens with a long scene in which Bert (who is at the table with his cap on and a magazine propped up in front of him) eats, drinks and reads, without uttering a word, while Rose prattles on about the food she's giving him and how cold it is outside and how lucky they are to have such a nice room. By talking in the way she does, she's giving herself the reassurance he refuses her. If she asks a question, she either answers it herself or goes on about something else without giving him time to answer, even if he wanted to. But she knows he doesn't and she's basically insulting him in exactly the same way that he's insulting her: by ignoring him. Talking to him all the time, she disregards his refusal to react, which is itself a reaction. She treats him like a little boy, telling him to put on a thick jersey, and she tells him what he thinks and feels, as if she knows better than he does. Her existence is centered on his but in effect she is denying him the right or the ability to exist independently.

In many ways her behavior corresponds to what Ronald Laing, in *The Self and Others*, calls "schizophrenogenic"—i.e., liable to undermine the man's confidence in his own emotional reactions and his own perception of reality. Bert gives no sign of being vulnerable and Pinter gives no sign of being interested in whether he is or not, but Rose's behavior pattern is almost exactly the same as Meg's in *The Birthday Party* and the mother's in *A Night Out*. In each case, the woman wants to keep the man in the house, in her sphere of influence, and in her routine, although she pretends not to mind whether he goes out.

> I haven't been out. I haven't been so well. I didn't feel up to it. Still, I'm much better today. I don't know about you though. I don't know whether you ought to go out. I mean, you shouldn't, straight after you've been laid up. Still. Don't worry, Bert. You go. You won't be long.

Then a minute later:

> I don't know why you have to go out. Couldn't you run it down tomorrow? I could put the fire

in later. You could sit by the fire. That's what you like, Bert, of an evening. It'll be dark in a minute as well, soon.

From the very first line of her monologue, there is great emphasis on the cold, the dark, and the dangers of the world outside compared to the safety and comfort of the room. Rose isn't only afraid of the world outside the house but nervous about other people in other rooms. She doesn't know whether anyone has moved into the basement and obviously hopes that no one has.

I don't know who lives down there now. Whoever it is, they're taking a big chance. Maybe they're foreigners.

Having established her insecurity, Pinter meticulously builds up an atmosphere of uncertainty and vagueness around her and around the room. The room itself is unambiguous—it's like the here-and-now, we can see it—but we don't know which floor it's on and Mr. Kidd doesn't know how many floors there are in the house; also we don't know for sure whether Mr. Kidd is the landlord or not. Rose says he is but Mr. and Mrs. Sands say he isn't. Mr. Kidd also contradicts himself about whether the house is full or not, and he's evasive about which room he lives in himself. At one time he used to live in this room, but he won't say, or doesn't remember, how long ago that was. The elaborate vagueness about time and place is very reminiscent of *Waiting for Godot*, and so is the rhythm of the dialogue with its staccato and its monosyllables.

MRS. SANDS: Why don't you sit down, Mrs.—

ROSE: Hudd. No thanks.

MR. SANDS: What did you say?

ROSE: When?

MR. SANDS: What did you say the name was?

ROSE: Hudd.

MR. SANDS: That's it. You're the wife of the bloke you mentioned then?

MR. SANDS: No, she isn't. That was Mr. Kidd.

MR. SANDS: Was it? I thought it was Hudd.

MR. SANDS: No, it was Kidd. Wasn't it, Mrs. Hudd?

ROSE: That's right. The landlord.

MRS. SANDS: No, not the landlord. The other man.

ROSE: Well, that's his name. He's the landlord.

MR. SANDS: Who?

ROSE: Mr. Kidd.

   (Pause.)

MR. SANDS: Is he?

MRS. SANDS: Maybe there are two landlords.

   (Pause.)

MR. SANDS: That'll be the day.

MRS. SANDS: What did you say?

MR. SANDS: I said that'll be the day.

   (Pause.)

ROSE: What's it like out?

MRS. SANDS: It's very dark out.

MR. SANDS: No darker than in.

MRS. SANDS: He's right there.

MR. SANDS: It's darker in than out, for my money.

The repetitiousness, the short and sometimes meaning-ful names (like Kidd), and the way the dialogue tacks back on itself obviously owe a great deal to

Beckett, and Pinter has acknowledged the influence. But he starts to develop a distinctive style of his own in which the questions and answers don't meet each other squarely. Quite apart from the comic effect, the way that the characters continue their own lines of thought shows us what their preoccupations are.

> ROSE: Well, it's a shame you have to go out in this weather, Mr. Kidd. Don't you have a help?
>
> MR. KIDD: Eh?
>
> ROSE: I thought you had a woman to help.
>
> MR. KIDD: I haven't got any woman.
>
> ROSE: I thought you had one when we first came.
>
> MR. KIDD: No women here.
>
> ROSE: Maybe I was thinking of somewhere else.
>
> MR. KIDD: Plenty of women round the corner. Not here though. Oh no. Eh, have I seen that before?
>
> ROSE: What?
>
> MR. KIDD: That.
>
> ROSE: I don't know. Have you?
>
> MR. KIDD: I seem to have some remembrance.
>
> ROSE: It's just an old rocking chair.
>
> MR. KIDD: Was it here when you came?
>
> ROSE: No, I brought it myself.
>
> MR. KIDD: I could swear blind I've seen that before.
>
> ROSE: Perhaps you have.
>
> MR. KIDD: What?
>
> ROSE: I say, perhaps you have.
>
> MR. KIDD: Yes, maybe I have.
>
> ROSE: Take a seat, Mr. Kidd.
>
> MR. KIDD: I wouldn't take an oath on it though.

It's also characteristic of Pinter to make the woman the spokesman for static security. What she voices is the desire to stay where she is in space and time. She is safe and satisfied with things as they are. When the blind Negro comes up from the basement, where he's been waiting for her with a message from her father, this is an invitation to make a movement back into the past. "Come home, Sal." The appearance of the blind Negro from the basement is more overtly symbolical than anything else in Pinter's work, although the meaning is open to any number of interpretations. Is the Negro the same man that Mr. and Mrs. Sands met in the dark and who told them that room Number 7 was vacant? Why does Rose start off by claiming that she doesn't know him and then seem to know that his name isn't Riley? And why does he call her Sal? (This is only the first of several instances in Pinter's plays where characters go by more than one name; it suggests that nothing is constant about their identity.) Why does Rose go blind when Bert kicks the Negro's head against the gas stove? This final episode in the play bristles with even more insoluble mysteries than the earlier episodes. Was Mr. Sands perching or sitting on the table? Why does Mrs. Sands object to this? Were the Sands going up or down the stairs when Rose opened the door of her room?

In each case the question is unanswerable on the evidence Pinter gives us, but in each case the fact that it's unanswerable contributes to the dramatic effect. This is a technique that Pinter went on using, but his ways of using it were soon to become much subtler.

The Dumb Waiter

The Dumb Waiter, Pinter's next one-act play, is a much more accomplished and relaxed piece of writing. The mystification is more controlled and the doors are open to much more comedy. The technique draws from both Beckett and music hall. Elaborate routines and stage business are mapped out and very funny dialogue is built up out of irrelevant scraps of information.

> *Gus ties his laces, rises, yawns and begins to walk slowly to the door, left. He stops, looks down, and shakes his foot.*
>
> *Ben lowers his paper and watches him. Gus kneels and unties his shoe-lace and slowly takes off the shoe. He looks inside it and brings out a flattened matchbox. He shakes it and examines it. Their eyes meet. Ben rattles his paper and reads. Gus puts the matchbox in his pocket and bends down to put on his shoe. He ties his lace,*

with difficulty. Ben lowers his paper and watches him. Gus walks to the door, left, stops, and shakes the other foot. He kneels, unties his shoelace, and slowly takes off the shoe. He looks inside it and brings out a flattened cigarette packet. He shakes it and examines it. Their eyes meet. Ben rattles his paper and reads. Gus puts the packet in his pocket, bends down, puts on his shoe and ties the lace . . .

BEN: Kaw!

    (He picks up the paper.)

  What about this? Listen to this!

    (He refers to the paper.)

  A man of eighty-seven wanted to cross the road. But there was a lot of traffic, see? He couldn't see how he was going to squeeze through. So he crawled under a lorry.

GUS: He what?

BEN: He crawled under a lorry. A stationary lorry.

GUS: No?

BEN: The lorry started and ran over him.

GUS: Go on!

BEN: That's what it says here.

GUS: Get away.

BEN: It's enough to make you want to puke, isn't it?

GUS: Who advised him to do a thing like that?

BEN: A man of eighty-seven crawling under a lorry!

GUS: It's unbelievable.

BEN: It's down here in black and white.

GUS: Incredible.

This is how the play begins: instead of planting points to get the plot going, Pinter is quite content to lean back and let the characters chat. He goes on to use the ball cock in the lavatory system, memories of football matches seen years ago and three-quarters forgotten, and more fragments read out of newspapers. But the comic touches aren't there just for their own sake. Underneath the casual surface, the components for an odd kind of plot are being assembled. We gather that Ben and Gus are here to do a job, but Pinter is in no hurry to let us know that they're professional killers. The crisp brightness of the comedy is being enjoyed in the unpleasant shadow of an impending climax of violence.

Again, the mystification contributes to the atmosphere and the flavor of what's going on. The men themselves seem to know comparatively little about the organization they're working for, though we never know quite how much they know. Complaining that there's no radio in the room, Gus says:

> He doesn't seem to bother much about our comfort these days.

But we have no idea who "he" is. "He" is rather like "they" in Beckett—the power that's responsible for making things the way they are and putting the protagonists into the situation that they're in, but anonymous and unfathomable.

In fact the whole conception of the play seems to owe a great deal to Beckett's novel *Molloy*. The pattern is the same—two men, one with authority over the other, in pursuit of a third man—and in both plots the quantity of unknown facts is overwhelming. Moran, the "agent" in *Molloy*, knows little about the organization that he's working for, and much of the comedy hinges on the discrepancy between the gravity of the mission (vague though it is) and the triviality of the distractions that get in the way of carrying it out. In *The Dumb Waiter*, Ben and Gus know what they have to do, but they don't know why, they don't know who their victims are and they don't know what advantage their deaths are to the organization that employs them. But the curiosity they show is fairly perfunctory: we don't feel that they really want to know any more than they do.

> Gus: Who clears up after we've gone? I'm curious about that. Who does the clearing up? Maybe they don't clear up. Maybe they just leave them there, eh? What do you think? How many jobs have we done? Blimey, I can't count them. What if they never clear anything up after we've gone.
> Ben (*pityingly*): You mutt. Do you think we're the only branch of this organization? Have a bit of common. They got departments for everything.
> Gus: What cleaners and all?
> Ben: You birk!

Their willingness to obey orders without inquiring into the mysteries behind them is bizarrely but amusingly underlined when the dumb waiter of the title starts to work. At first it had seemed that the room, as in *The Room*, was a place for resting and safety. But when the matches are slid underneath the door, Ben and Gus know that they are not alone in the house. Later, when they suddenly hear a loud clattering sound in the wall between the beds, they panic and grab their revolvers—and then the tension is punctured beautifully when the two men read the piece of paper they take out of the dumb waiter.

> GUS: Two braised steak and chips. Two sago puddings. Two teas without sugar.
> BEN: Let me see that. (*He takes the paper.*)
> GUS (*To himself*): Two teas without sugar.

The gunmen's pathetic efforts to obey the orders that come out of the shaft provide some moments of high comedy, especially when they reply to the demand for "Macaroni Pastitisio" and "Ormitha Macarounada" with three McVitie and Price biscuits, a packet of Lyons Red Label tea, a packet of Smith's Crisps and an Eccles cake, a half-pint of milk and a bar of Cadbury's fruit and nut chocolate. (Pinter shares the pleasure Beckett takes in cataloguing details into lists.) The situation is as bizarre as anything in *The Room*, but the symbolism is much less insistent. In a sense, the man who remains unseen and gives orders from above becomes God-like, especially when Ben and Gus send up all they have, and he still isn't satisfied. But there is enough comedy to prevent the symbolism from overbalancing the play, and the unsolved mysteries don't prevent the final twist (it turns out that Gus is to be the victim) from being neat and theatrically satisfying.

The Birthday Party

The Birthday Party was presented in May 1958 by Michael Codron at the Lyric, Hammersmith, where it bewildered the critics of the daily papers and had already closed before the *Sunday Times* appeared with a glowing review by Harold Hobson. "Mr. Pinter, on the evidence of this work, possesses the most original, disturbing and arresting talent in theatrical London." The play was revived in May 1959 by the Tavistock Repertory Company at the Tower Theatre. Thanks to the magazine *Encore* this amateur production was seen by a great many people who would otherwise have missed it, and it helped to turn the tide in Pinter's direction. Pinter himself pronounced the production better than the Hammersmith one. Certainly it was better than his own very slow production of the play for the Royal Shakespeare Theatre in June 1964.

This work has more substance than either of his other full-length plays. The impact is enormous; its moments of terror and violence are the best Pinter has contrived, and its structure is the most impressive he's yet achieved. The parts all contribute to the whole and the comedy blends well with the serious statements. The mystification is there, as always, but it doesn't interfere with the precision and clarity of the pattern.

It has been objected that Goldberg and McCann are less realistic than the other characters. Certainly they're less rooted into the realistic context of the shabby seaside boardinghouse, and certainly they're more mysterious than Meg and Petey and Lulu, because we don't know what they're at. Like Ben and Gus, they are two agents working for some organization we know nothing about, but although their mission and its motives remain mysterious, their language and their behavior merge perfectly well into the rest of the play.

Stanley, who is clearly a "naturalistic character" in that he isn't sent from another world, as they seem to be, is in fact just as impenetrable as Ben and Gus. Except for what we see of his lethargy, we are given no idea what has made him into the failure he is today. We know very little about his past, except for the hints of some estrangement from his father, but, like Goldberg and McCann, he is convincing without being entirely understandable. Like all Pinter's characters, he exists entirely through what he says and does on stage, but this existence is quite sufficient.

The beginning of the play is very much like that of *The Room*, with Petey sitting at the breakfast table with a paper, while Meg prattles on with her suffocating mixture of motherly attentiveness and self-praise. She seems to think her cornflakes are nicer than anybody else's. When Stanley, the substitute child for this childless mother, comes down, late, to breakfast, the flirty game that Meg plays with him is full of the affectionate insults that Pinter is so good at writing.

> MEG (*shyly*): Am I really succulent?
> STANLEY: Oh, you are. I'd rather have you than a cold in the nose any day.
> MEG: You're just saying that.
> STANLEY (*violently*): Look, why don't you get this place cleared up! It's a pigsty. And another thing, what about my room? It needs sweeping. I need a new room!
> MEG (*sensual, stroking his arm*): Oh, Stan, that's a lovely room. I've had some lovely afternoons in that room.

But the enjoyment of this squalid idyll is shattered in the usual Pinterish way—the safety of the room is threatened by the prospect of intruders from the world outside. Stanley, like a child, is immediately scared when he hears that Meg is expecting visitors and he gets his own back by scaring her.

> STANLEY (*advancing*): They're coming today.
> MEG: Who?
> STANLEY: They're coming in a van.
> MEG: Who?
> STANLEY: And do you know what they've got in that van?
> MEG: What?
> STANLEY: They've got a wheelbarrow in that van.
> MEG (*breathlessly*): They haven't.

STANLEY: Oh yes they have.

MEG: You're a liar.

STANLEY (*advancing upon her*): A big wheel-barrow. And when the van stops they wheel it out, and they wheel it up the garden path, and then they knock at the front door.

MEG: They don't.

STANLEY: They're looking for someone.

MEG: They're not.

STANLEY: They're looking for someone. A certain person.

MEG (*hoarsely*): No, they're not!

STANLEY: Shall I tell you who they're looking for?

MEG: No!

This is almost like a prophecy of doom in a Greek tragedy. We have no idea whether Stanley has any reason for being so anxious, but the dialogue builds up the expectation that something pretty nasty is going to happen.

The scene with Meg contains several indications of Stanley's immaturity. He puts up with her fussy mothering, which even goes to the extreme of asking him "Did you pay a visit this morning?" He obviously wants to do nothing but lie in bed and sit indoors, like a child afraid of going to school. His scene with Lulu carries the suggestion of immaturity still further. The girl is obviously interested in him, in spite of her complaints about his not washing or shaving, but he turns down the chance she gives him of going out with her. He doesn't want to go out at all.

The Stanley-Lulu scene is followed by the first scene with Goldberg and McCann—the Jew and the Irishman of the traditional joke. Goldberg's character immediately makes a very strong impact. He talks about himself with all the self-satisfaction of a self-made man, and he hands out glib advice to anyone who will listen—or seem to—with a vulgarly paternal expansiveness.

> GOLDBERG: Sit back, McCann. Relax. What's the matter with you? I bring you down for a few days to the seaside. Take a holiday. Do yourself a favour. Learn to relax, McCann, or you'll never get anywhere.
>
> McCANN: Ah sure I do try, Nat.
>
> GOLDBERG (*sitting at the table, right*): The secret is breathing. Take my tip. It's a well-known fact. Breathe in, breathe out, take a chance, let yourself go. What can you lose? Look at me. When I was an apprentice yet, McCann, every second Friday of the month my Uncle Barney used to take me to the seaside, regular as clockwork. Brighton, Canvey Island, Rottingdean—Uncle Barney wasn't particular. After lunch on Shabbuss we'd go and sit in a couple of deck-chairs— you know, the ones with canopies—we'd have a little paddle, we'd watch the tide coming in, going out, the sun coming down—golden days, believe me, McCann. (*Reminiscent.*) Uncle Barney. Of course, he was an impeccable dresser. One of the old school. He had a house just outside Basingstoke at the time. Respected by the whole community. Culture? Don't talk to me about culture. He was an all-round man, what do you mean? He was a cosmopolitan.

The inconsequentiality, the enjoyment of place-names, the cheap joviality, the accuracy of the Jewish rhythms, and the proud and pointless storytelling about relations or acquaintances are typical of Pinter. So far as his manner of speaking is concerned, Goldberg might have been created by any of the Jewish writers—even Wolf Mankowitz—but the association of the familiar manner with the obscure function is characteristic of Pinter. We don't know whether Stanley is going to be killed or not, but the way Goldberg speaks about "doing the job" reminds us of the two gunmen in *The Dumb Waiter*, while the way he speaks about how he was given the job is reminiscent of *Molloy*.

> GOLDBERG: And then this job came up out of the blue. Naturally they approached me to take care of it. And you know who I asked for?
> McCANN: Who?
> GOLDBERG: You.

As in *The Dumb Waiter*, the build-up of mystification develops a suspense which knocks the comedy into a minor key and, again as in *The Dumb Waiter*, the symbolism is redeemed from crudeness by its effectiveness in providing comic relief from the suspense. Meg's birthday present of a toy drum has several different kinds of significance. It sums up the old woman's attitude to the substitute son who can't bear her but hasn't got the strength to escape. Like Rose's chatter to Bert, Meg's fussy attentiveness shows the wish to give and receive attention, combined with an insulting reduction of the grown man to the status of a little boy. The present of a toy is an ingenuous attempt to give to the failed musician something that will make up for his not having a piano, and in giving it she ingenuously asks for a kiss. Stanley's shoulders sag as he complies. To please her, he puts the drum round his neck and beats it, marching round the table. But he loses control and starts banging it frantically as the curtain comes down on Act One.

Act Two, it is clear, will culminate in the actual party, but the suspense is built up slowly before we get to it. Some of the things that happen are not at all sinister in themselves but they all add to the accumulation of tensions which will have to break, like a storm, before the play is over. Seemingly to amuse himself, McCann tears a sheet of newspaper into vertical strips, and then, when Stanley isn't allowed to touch the paper, we can't help wondering why. Stanley's scene with McCann is full of hidden menace, with odd little touches like having each of them whistle alternate snatches of a tune while the other speaks, so that the whistling is continuous through several lines of dialogue. When Stanley tries to leave, McCann forces him to stay, without actually using any violence, but by indicating that he will if necessary. Stanley's guilt and anxiety are very cleverly sketched in, creating some doubt in our minds about whether Goldberg and McCann are intrinsically dangerous to him or, like the matchseller, in *A Slight Ache*, only dangerous because he thinks they are. He first makes a pathetic effort to convince McCann that he isn't the man they're looking for. When that fails, he tries to make a friend of him. He also tries to get rid of Goldberg by pretending to be the manager of the boardinghouse and saying they don't have a room for him.

The scene of rapid-fire questioning seems to owe

something to a rather unlikely source: *Johnson Over Jordan*, by J. B. Priestley, which contains a long scene in which the hero is quizzed by two Examiners.

> JOHNSON (*sinking fast now*): Look here, gentlemen, all I can say is—I've tried to do my best.
>
> 2ND EXAMINER (*going right up to him, in smooth deadly tone*): Possibly. But is your best good enough?
>
> 1ST EXAMINER (*with the same horrible technique*): After all, what do you *know?*
>
> 2ND EXAMINER (*severe again now*): How far have you tried to acquaint yourself with the findings of chemistry, physics, biology, astronomy, mathematics?
>
> 1ST EXAMINER: Ask yourself what you know about the Mendelian Law, the Quantum Theory, Spectral Analysis, or the behaviour of Electrons and Neutrons.
>
> 2ND EXAMINER: Could you explain Freud's theory of the Id, Marx's Surplus Value, Neo-Realism, Non-representational Art, Polyphonic Music?
>
> 1ST EXAMINER: Or—give an exact account of the sequence of events leading up to the outbreak of war in 1914?
>
> 2ND EXAMINER (*with dangerous easiness*): You were taught French at school?
>
> JOHNSON: Yes.
>
> 2ND EXAMINER (*turning like a tiger*): Have you ever brushed up your French?

The scene in *The Birthday Party* screws the tension still tighter, by making more use of rhythm. But the humor in the lines, which cuts deliberately against the grimness of the bullying, is very reminiscent of the Priestley passage.

> GOLDBERG: When did you come to this place?
> STANLEY: Last year.
> GOLDBERG: Where did you come from?
> STANLEY: Somewhere else.
> GOLDBERG: Why did you come here?
> STANLEY: My feet hurt!
> GOLDBERG: Why did you stay?
> STANLEY: I had a headache!
> GOLDBERG: Did you take anything for it?
> STANLEY: Yes.
> GOLDBERG: What?
> STANLEY: Fruit salts!
> GOLDBERG: Enos or Andrews?
> STANLEY: En—An—
> GOLDBERG: Did you stir properly? Did they fizz?
> STANLEY: Now, now, wait, you—
> GOLDBERG: Did they fizz? Did they fizz or didn't they fizz?
> McCANN: He doesn't know!
> GOLDBERG: You don't know. What's happened to your memory, Webber? When did you last have a bath?
> STANLEY: I have one every—
> GOLDBERG: Don't lie.
> McCANN: You betrayed the organization. I know him!

The tension is wound up tighter and tighter until it breaks, as it is bound to, into violence. But it isn't the violence we expect. Instead of attacking Stanley, Goldberg is attacked by him, kicked in the stomach, and from the floor he tries to restrain McCann from avenging the blow with a chair he's picked up. As McCann and Stanley face each other, circling, the question is still open whether in cross-questioning Stanley, Goldberg and McCann have been doing anything more sinister than teasing him. Then the scene is interrupted by an offstage drumbeat. Meg is coming down the stairs in evening dress playing Stanley's toy drum. So now the conflict is forced back out of the open, and the menace of impending violence is concealed under the surface of conviviality, as the oddly assorted characters celebrate the birthday party, with Stanley still protesting that it isn't his birthday—a typical Pinter ambiguity.

From its crude presentation in *The Room*, the symbolism of darkness is refined and used with much more theatrical purpose. Stanley can see very little without his glasses, which McCann has snatched off during the interrogation. They are given back to him, but later they are to be broken deliberately. The effect of plunging the stage into darkness and illuminating one face with the beam of a flashlight is used twice, and after a significant game of blindman's buff, the stage is in darkness for about two minutes except for a moment when the flashlight goes on. Grunts from McCann and Goldberg, the noise of a stick banging on the side of the drum, and whimpers from Lulu all add to the terror. The build-ups are extremely effective, and again when the climaxes of violence come they are not what we expect. At each point of violence or near violence, it is Stanley, seemingly so unaggressive, who is the attacker, and it is a woman who is the victim. Before the blackout, blindfold and baited by McCann, with his glasses broken and one foot caught in the broken drum,

Stanley tries to strangle Meg. And in the final climax of the act, Lulu is spreadeagled on the table with Stanley bent over her until Goldberg and McCann drive him off. Unfortunately the grudge against women never quite comes into focus either in Stanley or in Pinter.

After the suspense, the claustrophobic theatricality, and the concentrated multilevel meaningfulness of Act Two, Act Three is something of a letdown. The long opening scene between Meg and Petey is lacking in tension, and without any redeeming comedy. A little suspense is supplied by the big car waiting outside and by the information that Stanley has had a "nervous breakdown." The signs are that Goldberg and McCann have got hold of him and that Petey and Meg are powerless to get him out of their clutches. But this is not enough. It is effective when McCann has qualms about going back upstairs into the room where Stanley is, and there's a nasty threat in the mention of "Monty," a friend of Goldberg's, as the doctor best suited to treat Stanley. But altogether the writing lacks the sureness of touch it had in Act Two. There are some comic moments in the scene between Goldberg and McCann, with McCann peering into Goldberg's mouth. The latter, who has been bragging about his health, emits a high-pitched wheeze-whine, which makes him look round as though somebody else had done it. But Pinter doesn't really find his feet until the very funny scene between Lulu and Goldberg.

> LULU (*with growing anger*): You used me for
> a night. A passing fancy.
> GOLDBERG: Who used who?

LULU: You made use of me by cunning when my defences were down.

GOLDBERG: Who took them down?

LULU: That's what you did. You quenched your ugly thirst. You took advantage of me when I was overwrought. I wouldn't do those things again, not even for a Sultan!

GOLDBERG: One night doesn't make a harem.

LULU: You taught me things a girl shouldn't know before she's been married at least three times!

GOLDBERG: Now you're a jump ahead! What are you complaining about?

The appearance of Stanley provides a very good moment. He is clean-shaven now and dressed in a black jacket and striped trousers; a bowler hat is in his hand. (One interpreter concluded that the play was about the conformist pressures of society.) But he can't speak now, only make inarticulate sounds. Goldberg and McCann's scene with him is much less effective than the one in Act Two. The rhythm is strong and the language seems to derive from T. S. Eliot's verse plays—*The Family Reunion* in particular.

GOLDBERG: From now on, we'll be the hub of your wheel.

MCCANN: We'll renew your season ticket.

GOLDBERG: We'll take tuppence off your morning tea.

MCCANN: We'll give you a discount on all inflammable goods.

GOLDBERG: We'll watch over you.

MCCANN: Advise you.

In the end they take him away in the car. Petey, who is one of Pinter's few sympathetic characters, tries to stop them, but he's weak and easily scared off by the invitation to come with them. The play ends, as it began, with Meg and Petey alone together, in the room.

A Slight Ache

A Slight Ache was conceived as a radio play.
Commissioned by the BBC for the Third Programme,
it was broadcast in July 1959, and was not staged
until eighteen months later at the Arts. This is the
first of Pinter's plays in which the action isn't confined
to a single room, but even radio didn't entice him
any further afield than the garden, and all the in-
terior action is set in different rooms of the same
house. Once again the theme is the threat of the intruder from outside, and once again Pinter explores
the dramatic potential of silence. But this time it's
something different from the silence of the man in
face of the nagging woman and from the inarticulate-
ness of the defeated Stanley. In effect, the matchseller's silence is a destructive weapon which enables
him to dispossess Edward of both his wife and home.
The question of whether this was his intention doesn't
come into the picture. Just as *The Birthday Party* refused to concern itself with whether Stanley's guilt

feelings contributed to his undoing, so, in *A Slight Ache*, the matchseller is shown as entirely passive, nothing more than a screen for Edward and Flora to project on. The old man does nothing to set them against each other; what happens is entirely their doing.

On the air, silence is almost tantamount to non-existence—a point that Beckett exploits in his radio plays—and in the broadcast of *A Slight Ache*, the reality of the matchseller was in doubt. Obviously he isn't a fantasy because Edward and Flora both see him and speak to him and Flora feels him; but far from having a clear physical appearance, he seems to Edward to change shape and size.* Sometimes he looks strong, sometimes weak, and to Flora he is sometimes repulsive, sometimes attractive. In the television production (BBC-2, February 1967, directed by Christopher Morahan), the matchseller was effective so long as the camera was behind him, but the close-ups of the one-eyed actor's face all jarred. His nonreaction is far better left to a face we can't see, or can't see clearly.

Edward and Flora belong to a higher social class than any of Pinter's earlier characters. They both take considerable pride in their activities, she in her garden, he in his writing, and with both of them, Pinter picks on the right significant details to make the social setting real—the canopy, that Flora puts up in the garden for Edward to write under, the polo shorts, the convolvulus and the honeysuckle, and the gong sounded before meals. All these details are es-

---

* This is rather like the way Mr. Knott's appearance keeps changing in Beckett's *Watt*.

tablished by references to them—except in the television version, nothing of them is seen or heard by the audience. (For a radio play it has astonishingly few sound effects.) The pride and social superiority of Edward and Flora are necessary to make their humiliation all the greater as they are broken down by the "harmless old man," although Edward's way of talking is made to sound slightly ridiculous right from the beginning. As the old man's silence drives him into more and more desperate straits in keeping up a one-sided conversation, we hear the anxiety behind the attempt to impress. The clichés clash against the strenuous efforts to present himself as an original, and the facts come to sound very much like fiction.

> Yes, I . . . I was in much the same position myself then as you are now, you understand. Struggling to make my way in the world. I was in commerce too. (*With a chuckle.*) Oh, yes, I know what it's like—the weather, the rain, beaten from pillar to post, up hill and down dale . . . the rewards were few . . . winters in hovels . . . up till all hours working at your thesis . . . yes, I've done it all. Let me advise you. Get a good woman to stick by you. Never mind what the world says. Keep at it. Keep your shoulder to the wheel. It'll pay dividends.

In his second scene with the old man, Edward gives away so much of himself that there is no chance left of holding on to any kind of pride. From thinking the old man is laughing at him, he sees that he's crying.

> You're weeping. You're shaking with grief. For me. I can't believe it. For my plight. I've been wrong.

Which leads him on to give away still more of himself, until he realizes, with horror, that the man is actually laughing.*

The one element in Edward's humiliation which does not quite fall into place is the mysterious "slight ache" of the title. It seems to be something that affects his vision, although he denies that he has any difficulty in seeing and refuses to let Flora bathe his eyes. But he starts sneezing in his second scene with the matchseller.

> Ah. Fever. Excuse me. (*He blows his nose.*) I've caught a cold. A germ. In my eyes. It was this morning. In my eyes. My eyes. (*Pause. He falls to the floor.*)

Apart from this, his confessions are well-written, and in the production at the Arts, Emlyn Williams made his self-inflicted downfall very effective.

The changes in Flora are less convincing. Pinter has less sympathy for her and uses her scenes with the matchseller to indulge his predilection for spotting the tart in the lady. In Edward's scenes, we see exactly how each step leads to the next. In Flora's, Pinter shows no real interest in what takes her from contempt to desire. Or, perhaps what interests him is the fact that there is nothing there to cause the transition.

> Really, I think you'd amuse me if you weren't so hideous. You're probably quite amusing in your own way. (*Seductively.*) Tell me all about

---

* All this works far better if the uncertainty is entirely Edward's. If we see the man's face, it is ours too.

love. Speak to me of love. (*Pause.*) God knows what you're saying at this very moment. It's quite disgusting. Do you know when I was a girl I loved . . . I loved . . . I simply adored . . . what *have* you got on, for goodness sake? A jersey? It's clogged. Have you been rolling in mud? (*Slight pause.*) You haven't been rolling in mud, have you? (*She rises and goes over to him.*) And what have you got under your jersey? Let's see. (*Slight pause.*) I'm not tickling you, am I? No. Good . . . Lord, is this a vest? That's quite original. Quite original. (*She sits on the arms of his chair.*) Hmmnn, you're solid old boy, I must say. Not at all like a jelly. All you need is a bath. A lovely lathery bath. And a good scrub. A lovely lathery scrub. (*Pause.*) Don't you? It will be a pleasure. (*She throws her arms round him.*) I'm going to keep you.

In the way that affection suddenly emerges, like a threat, this is very much like Ruth's surprise declaration to Lenny in *The Homecoming*.

If you take the glass . . . I'll take you.

In both cases, the surprise is something of a strain on the credulity. It's easy to believe that both women are capable of betraying their men, but it's hard to believe in it as happening in the way Pinter makes it happen. The endings of *The Room, The Dumb Waiter, The Birthday Party,* and *A Night Out* all have an absolute rightness. They are perfectly consistent with the illogical logic of the play. But to make Flora leave Edward with the matchseller's tray is straining too hard to contrive a neat pattern. In the television production—no doubt with Pinter's ap-

proval, since it couldn't have been done without—
this ending was cut and the play ended with Edward
prostrate on the floor and the matchseller stepping
over him as Flora was about to show him over the
house, *his* house, she now calls it.

The other element in the play which is unsatisfy-
ing is the relationship between the protracted wasp-
killing episode at the beginning and the matchseller
episode that takes up the rest of the action. It may be
that no relationship is intended, but that doesn't
mean that no relationship is necessary. Or it may be
that a contrast is intended between the reaction of
Edward and Flora to the wasp, which they destroy
because it frightens them, and to the matchseller,
whom they see as a "harmless old man." The wasp
killing is theatrically quite effective in itself and useful in establishing Flora and Edward, but the relationship of the two parts of the play to each other
and to the "slight ache" remains unsatisfactory.

A Night Out

A *Night Out*, Pinter's next play, which was broadcast in March 1960 and televised a month later, moves about freely from one location to another. This time the immature hero rebels against his dominating mother by making two attempts in one evening to escape from the comforts and the safety of home life. Both times he fails and returns.

The play begins in the same way as *The Birthday Party*, with the woman calling the man's name and the man not answering. As always, the loquacious motherly fussing produces evasiveness in the male.

> MOTHER: Albert, I've been calling you. (*She watches him.*) What are you doing?
> ALBERT: Nothing.
> MOTHER: Didn't you hear me call you, Albert? I've been calling you from upstairs.
> ALBERT: You seen my tie?
> MOTHER: Oh, I say, I'll have to put the flag out.

ALBERT: What do you mean?

MOTHER: Cleaning your shoes, Albert? I'll have to put the flag out, won't I?

Albert is twenty-eight, but he behaves as though he were much younger, putting up with a mother who tries to use him one-sidedly in a relationship entirely determined by her needs.

MOTHER: You promise?

ALBERT: Promise what?

MOTHER: That . . . that you won't upset your father.

ALBERT: My father? How can I upset my father? You're always talking about upsetting people who are dead!

MOTHER: Oh, Albert, you don't know how you hurt me, you don't know the hurtful way you've got, speaking of your poor father like that.

As a character, though, the mother doesn't come off as well as Meg. Pinter tends to be better when writing about mother-substitutes rather than actual mothers. His best mother-substitute of all is the father in the all-male household in *The Homecoming*.

The second scene in *A Night Out* is at a coffee counter, and, as in *The Dumb Waiter*, Pinter enjoys himself with a conversation about football, writing this time from the viewpoint of the players. Albert, we soon gather, has let the side down.

KEDGE: He's a good ball-player, that Connor, isn't he?

SEELEY: Look. I said to Albert before the kick-off, Connor's on the right wing, I said, play your normal game. I told him six times before the kick-off.

KEDGE: What's the good of him playing his normal game? He's a left half, he's not a left back.

SEELEY: Yes, but he's a defensive left half, isn't he? That's why I told him to play his normal game. You don't want to worry about Connor, I said, he's a good ball-player but he's not all that good.

KEDGE: Oh, he's good, though.

SEELEY: No one's denying he's good. But he's not all that good. I mean, he's not tip-top. You know what I mean?

KEDGE: He's fast.

SEELEY: He's fast, but he's not all that fast, is he?

KEDGE (*doubtfully*): Well, not all that fast . . .

Albert arrives late, having had difficulty in getting away from the mother, who's been trying to make herself indispensable to him. She delays his departure by insisting on brushing his suit, straightening his tie, and giving him a clean handkerchief for his breast pocket. When he finally appears, Albert shows himself to be insecure about girls, not really keen, after all, to go to the party, and very nettled when one of the boys inquires maliciously about his mother's health. This prepares us for the outbreak of violence at the party. The others all resent Albert because he's so quiet, and he's baited by the boys, led on by the girls, and finally blamed for an incident when one of the girls screams. In fact it is the old man in whose honor the party is being given who touches her. Again, as in *The Birthday Party*, the fighting is started by the least aggressive character on stage. The weapon of the aggressor is words and the physical violence comes only when the victim breaks. The line that makes Albert hit out at the ringleader of his enemies is "You're a mother's boy."*

Returning home, Albert is at once the object of another bullying verbal attack from his mother. She accuses him of "mucking about with girls," complains about the state of his clothes, refuses to believe he's been at the firm's party, informs him that he hasn't eaten anything all evening so he must have his dinner, reproaches him for not bringing home a really nice girl and introducing her, remonstrates about the high hopes his father had for him, and praises herself for keeping such a lovely home. However, her chief complaint is:

> Not for years, not for years, have you come up to me and said, Mum, I love you, like you did when you were a little boy. You've never said it without me having to ask you. Not since before your father died.

Again Albert is provoked into aggression. He seizes the clock from the table and raises it above his head to hit her. And again he goes out.

But the tart who picks him up turns out to be just as fussy and irritating as the mother. She's one of Pinter's essays in lower-class snobbery, and he holds the balance very well between what is virtually a monologue from her and Albert's one-word reactions.

---

* In the second television production, directed by Christopher Morahan on BBC-2 in February 1967, Albert punches Seeley by mistake and apologizes to him.

The tart talks proudly about the aristocratic features of the little girl in the photograph on the mantelpiece, saying it's her daughter, although actually it's herself when young. She lies about the smart boarding school the little girl is at, complains that the neighborhood is "full of people of no class at all," and doesn't allow Albert to swear, to sit in her chair, or to drop ashes on the carpet. She even attacks the morality of other girls, though she's curious to know how far they go. Again, the meek man is provoked into violence, dropping a lighted cigarette on her carpet and using force to keep her away when she goes to pick it up. Albert is now the dangerous intruder in somebody else's room. Terrorizing her into silence by threatening her with the clock, he revenges himself for her monologue by having one of his own in which, incoherently, all his grievances about his mother and about the party come out in one long stream of protest.

> ALBERT: You're all the same, you see, you're all the same, you're just a dead weight round my neck. What makes you think . . . What makes you think you can . . . tell me . . . It's the same as this business about the light in Grandma's room. Always something. Always something. (*To her.*) My ash? I'll put it where I like! You see this clock? Watch your step. Just watch your step.
>
> GIRL: Stop this. What are you—?
>
> ALBERT (*seizing her wrist, with trembling, controlled violence*): Watch your step! (*Stammering.*) I've had—I've had—I've had—just about enough. Get it? . . . You know what I did? . . . I'm just telling you, that's all. (*Breathlessly.*) You haven't got any breeding.

> She hadn't either. And what about those girls
> tonight? Same kind. And that one. I didn't
> touch her!

Once he's made her knuckle under to his will
power, he celebrates in the same way as Wally does
with the girl in *Night School*—by giving her orders.
He makes her walk to the wall, cover her face, pick
her shoes up, and put them on. Like Wally and Stanley, he doesn't know what he wants from the girl,
and he leaves without sleeping with her. He goes
home to find his mother offended but unhurt. In fact
he hadn't hit her: the impression we got that he had
was a piece of cheating, easy to bring off on radio
and television* but harder to bring off on stage. The
ultimate humiliation for Albert and the ultimate sign
of the lack of contact between them is the mother's
forgiveness.

> Listen, Albert, I'll tell you what I'm going to
> do. I'm going to forget all about it . . . We'll
> have your holiday in a fortnight. We can go
> away. (*She strokes his hand.*) We'll go away
> . . . together.

---

* Christopher Morahan's production didn't attempt to give
the impression that Albert hit his mother. We saw his arm
frozen in the air with the clock raised threateningly, but
it was obvious that threat wouldn't be carried out before
the picture faded. This took a lot of the force out of Albert's "You know what I did?" in the scene with the tart,
and a lot of the tension out of the whole scene, because
we no longer thought of Albert as having come out of the
house because his mother was lying there unconscious.

The Caretaker

The Caretaker is an easier play to "understand" than The Birthday Party—though not without its mystifications and its obscurities—and the London production boasted a brilliant performance by Donald Pleasence, which helped to make it a commercial success. But what helped still more was the fact that Pinter's name was very much in fashion by then.

Not that the play didn't deserve its long run. Within its limits—and basically it's only a one-act play teased out into a more usable length—it's often very funny, very effective and even moving. As a character, Davies comes off as well in the writing as he did in Pleasence's performance, but Pinter doesn't achieve anything like the same success with either of the brothers. Aston is more fully realized than Mick, partly because the room is an extension of his personality. He's compulsive about accumulating objects from junk shops—cupboards, boxes, vases, drawers, tools, ornaments, chairs and all the assorted lumber that gives the room its special atmosphere. It is also, one gathers, the same feeling that "this might come in useful one day" which makes him pick up Davies. The compulsiveness, the vague goodwill, the hours-long lingering over petty household jobs like putting a plug on the toaster, the fumbling friendship with Davies, and the good intentions that will never take effect are all sketched in effectively.

Where the characterization fails is in its departure from Pinter's normal practice. Aston's long narrative speech at the end of Act Two, describing the episode in the mental hospital, has been highly praised by some critics, but it gives us information we don't need and clashes badly with the style of the writing all round it. Though Davies's speeches about his past may be fact or fiction or a mixture of the two, and while Mick's speeches are mostly fiction, Aston is giving us something that we are obviously meant to swallow whole. Worst of all, it comes across as oddly old-fashioned. Pinter knows as well as anyone how unnecessary it is to explain present behavior in terms of past history, but here he's doing just that.

But the partial failure with Aston is less serious than the failure with Mick, who is very effective when silent but often disastrous when he speaks. He provides an air of mystery and tension at the very beginning of the play by appearing and then going out when he hears the voices of the others approaching. He also provides all the violence and the suspense of the moments when he's terrorizing Davies or goading him into drawing his knife. He plays practical tricks on him in the dark, effectively enough, but the blackout he produces is nothing like so frightening as its prototype in *The Birthday Party*. It comes

at the beginning of one of the many short scenes in the play. Davies comes in, tries the light switch and can't make it work. He moves about, stumbling. He lights a match, but it goes out and he drops the box, which is kicked away. He gets scared and after talking to himself he starts shouting to the invisible intruder that he's got a knife. He stumbles, falls, cries out, and whimpers. Then in the silence, Mick starts the Electrolux, moving the nozzle along the floor. Davies skips away terrified and flattens himself against the wall, knife in hand. Switching the light on, Mick announces laconically that he was just doing some spring cleaning.

Episodes like this come off in exactly the way Pinter wants them to, but Mick's long speeches don't.

> You remind me of my uncle's brother. He was always on the move, that man. Never without his passport. Had an eye for the girls. Very much your build. Bit of an athlete. Long-jump specialist. He had a habit of demonstrating different run-ups in the drawing-room round about Christmas-time. Had a penchant for nuts. That's what it was. Nothing else but a penchant. Couldn't eat enough of them. Peanuts, walnuts, brazil nuts, monkey nuts, wouldn't touch a piece of fruit cake. Had a marvellous stop-watch. Picked it up in Hong Kong. The day after they chucked him out of the Salvation Army. Used to go in number four for Beckenham Reserves. That was before he got his Gold Medal. Had a funny habit of carrying his fiddle on his back. Like a papoose. I think there was a bit of the Red Indian in him. To be honest, I've never made out how he came to be my uncle's

brother. I've often thought that maybe it was the other way round. I mean that my uncle was his brother and he was my uncle. But I never called him uncle. As a matter of fact I called him Sid. My mother called him Sid too. It was a funny business. Your spitting image he was. Married a Chinaman and went to Jamaica.

The gratuitous reminiscing about relations is rather like Goldberg's, but the surreal touches look forward to *The Collection* and *The Homecoming*. But coming so soon after the violence that ended Act One—the action is continuous—the speech destroys a lot of the tension with its funny but free-wheeling irrelevancies. Mick's reactions to Davies are almost as confusing to us as they are to the old man. Basically it's clear that he's jealous of his brother's relationship with him and that he wants to get rid of him. But he goes to the most improbable lengths in order to do this. He alternates between scaring him and trying to make friends with him, so as to woo him away from Aston. He succeeds in getting Davies to come to him with complaints about his brother. That Mick should then turn against Davies is predictable and doesn't make any useful point. Altogether, Pinter's treatment of Mick seems to suffer from a lack of interest in him, except as a means of producing mystification and stage terror.

Davies is a very much more successful creation. Pinter obviously shares Beckett's interest in tramps, and he does very well with the two female tramps in "The Black and the White." Davies is the most fully rounded character in Pinter, and the characterization doesn't depend at all on giving us any information

about Davies's past. We gather that he's spent much
of his life on the road and that he's just been working
in the kitchen of a cafe, but otherwise we learn all we
need to know about him through what he says—and
above all through what he leaves unsaid. His evasiveness is given a rhythm in the dialogue which
Pleasence caught superbly in the performance.

> DAVIES: There's a caff down there, you see,
> might be able to get fixed up there. I was
> there, see? I know they were a bit short-
> handed. They might be in the need of a bit
> of staff.
>
> ASTON: When was that?
>
> DAVIES: Eh? Oh, well, that was . . . near on . . .
> that'll be . . . that'll be a little while ago now.
> But of course what it is, they can't find the
> right kind of people in these places. What
> they want to do, they're trying to do away
> with these foreigners, you see, in catering. I
> mean, that's what they're aiming at. That's
> one thing I know for a fact.
>
> ASTON: Hmmn.
>
> DAVIES: See, I was thinking, once I got down
> there, I might have a look in at the stadium,
> at Wembley Stadium. For all the big matches,
> get my meaning? They need people down
> there to run the ground, see, to keep the
> ground. Or another thing I could do, I could
> go along down there to Kennington Oval. All
> these big sports grounds, it stands to reason,
> they need people, to keep the ground, that's
> what they want, that's what they're crying
> out for. It's only common sense, en't? Oh, I
> got all that under way . . . that's . . . uh . . .
> that's . . . what I'll be doing.

A lifetime of procrastination is audible not only in the phrases but in the way they're joined together. But, like the tart in *A Night Out,* Davies is a great snob: "I've eaten dinner off the best of plates." He considers himself superior to the Indians who live next door and tries to blame them for the noises he's been making in his sleep. "I tell you what, maybe it were them Blacks." He claims to have left his wife because he found her dirty underwear in the vegetable pan, and he feels superior to Aston—at least *he's* never been in a mental hospital. Pinter extracts every ounce of comedy from Davies's incongruous vanities.

Once again there's a great deal of emphasis on the room and some mystery about who the landlord is. When Davies tries to find out, Aston is evasive, but implies that the house belongs to him. Mick later insists that it's his. And again, the script is very vague about the other rooms in the house. "They're out of commission," we are told. Nor do we ever find out where Mick sleeps now. But like Wally in *Night School,* he seems to be possessed by immature jealousy because someone else has been given the bed that used to be his; he also seems to be frightened of the old man, although Davies, apart from his smell, is obviously just as innocuous as the matchseller in *A Slight Ache.*

The other major success of the play is in exploring, comparing, and making so much capital out of the fantasies of two such off-beat characters as Davies and Aston—in linking them together into the context of the room. The collection of junk in the background is there all the time as an ironic visual counterpoint to everything Aston says about his plans for the house. We know that the things he thought would come in useful never will, we know that he will never mend the plug or build the shed or put up the partition.

> Once I get that shed up outside . . . I'll be able to give a bit more thought to the flat, you see. Perhaps I can knock up one or two things for it. (*He walks to the window.*) I can work with my hands, you see. That's one thing I can do. I never knew I could. But I can do all sorts of things now, with my hands. You know, manual things. When I get that shed up out there . . . I'll have a workshop, you see. I . . . could do a bit of woodwork. Simple woodwork, to start. Working with . . . good wood.
>   (*Pause.*)
> Of course, there's a lot to be done to this place. What I think, though, I think I'll put in a partition . . . in one of the rooms along the landing. I think it'll take it. You know . . . they've got these screens . . . you know . . . Oriental. They break up a room with them. Make it into two parts. I could either do that or I could have a partition. I could knock them up, you see, if I had a workshop.
>   (*Pause.*)
> Anyway, I think I've decided on the partition.

Aston's manner of speaking is quite adequately differentiated from Davies's, but there's something of the same rhythm of procrastination in both. The scenes between the two of them contain some of the vaguest dialogue that's ever been written, but it's precise enough in making its point about the speakers.

DAVIES: . . . I never been a caretaker before.
(Pause.)

ASTON: How do you feel about being one, then?

DAVIES: Well, I reckon . . . Well, I'd have to know . . . you know . . .

ASTON: What sort of . . .

DAVIES: Yes, what sort of . . . you know . . .
(Pause.)

ASTON: Well, I mean . . .

DAVIES: I mean, I'd have to . . . I'd have to . . .

ASTON: Well, I could tell you . . .

DAVIES: That's . . . that's it . . . you see . . . you get my meaning?

ASTON: When the time comes . . .

DAVIES: I mean, that's what I'm getting at, you see . . .

ASTON: More or less exactly what you . . .

DAVIES: You see, what I mean to say . . . what I'm getting at is . . . I mean, what sort of jobs . . .
(Pause.)

ASTON: Well, there's things like the stairs . . . and the . . . the bells . . .

DAVIES: But it'd be a matter . . . wouldn't it . . . it'd be a matter of a broom . . . isn't it?

ASTON: You could have a duster . . .

DAVIES: Oh, I know I could have that . . . but I couldn't manage without a . . . without a broom . . . could I?

ASTON: You'd have to have a broom . . .

DAVIES: That's it . . . that's just what I was thinking . . .

ASTON: I'd be able to pick one up for you, without much trouble . . . and of course, you'd . . . need a few brushes . . .

Donald Pleasence, center, as Davies in *The Caretaker* at
London's Arts Theatre, 1960. Peter Woodthorpe, left, as
Aston and Alan Bates as Mick.
MICHAEL BOYS

Leo McKern as the self-made tycoon, Robert Disson, and Vivien Merchant as Wendy, his somewhat menacing secretary, in the BBC-1 production of *Tea Party*.
BBC

Opposite: left to right: Derek Godfrey as Law, Kika Markham as Jane, and Harold Pinter as Stott in the BBC-2 production of *The Basement*.
BBC

Paul Rogers as Max bends over John Normington as Sam in the Royal Shakespeare production of *The Homecoming*. Ian Holm is Lenny.
DOMINIC

Barbara Tarbuck as Ellen in the 1970 production of *Silence* at the Lincoln Center's Forum Theater. Left and right: Robert Symonds as Rumsey and James Patterson as Bates.

MARTHA SWOPE

Robert Shaw as Deeley, Mary Ure as Kate, and Rosemary
Harris as Anna in *Old Times* as presented at the Billy Rose
Theater in 1971.
FRIEDMAN-ABELES

Opposite: Mildred Natwick as Beth and Robert Symonds
as Duff in *Landscape*, directed by Peter Gill and produced
at the Forum Theater in 1970.
MARTHA SWOPE

DAVIES: You'd need implements . . . you see
. . . you'd need a good few implements . . .

They are like two children, delighted at finding uses for the words they have picked up, but not really believing in the plans that they are making for the objects they have picked up. Somewhere, they know it's all a game. Pinter makes this clear without losing his sympathy for them.

If it had been a one-act play, centered on making this and the immediately relevant points, *The Caretaker* might have come off brilliantly. As it is, it's thin in places and padded out in others. The conversation about different kinds of saws, for instance, goes on too long, and some of the blackout lines are weak, repeating notes that have already been struck, instead of striking new ones. After writing so much for television, Pinter obviously found it easier to go on working in short scenes, but the discontinuity is sometimes distracting.

The failure with Mick is a curious one. He doesn't belong to the play in the same way that Aston and Davies do, and his fantasies, whatever they are, are not subject to the same scrutiny. His enjoyment of teasing Davies is obvious enough, and it's quite effective—and rather pathetic—when Davies falls so readily into the trap of complaining to him about Aston. After this, the end is predictable and inevitable. Davies has tried to join forces with his enemy against the man who has befriended him. In any case, he is the intruder in the room and he has to be thrown out. The parting between Aston and Davies at the end of the play has an odd kind of poignancy. But it doesn't leave us, as the end of *The Birthday Party* did, with a sense of solid experience behind us.

Night School

Night School is another play which started its life on the radio before being translated to television. This time the mother role is divided between two aunts, Annie and Milly. They have betrayed their nephew Wally by renting his room to a girl while he was serving a prison sentence, so that a struggle for possession of the room ensues on his return. He is offended to find that the girl has made his room effeminate.

> Look at those frills. Frills . . . all over the place. Bloody dolls' house. My damn room.

But he's not man enough to seize the chance of making a takeover bid for the room with her in it. Instead of letting her see him for what he really is, a very petty criminal, he puts on a hopeless act of being big. And instead of reacting to the real girl in front of him, he goes for help to a father-figure (the landlord) asking him to locate a girl from a photograph, without realizing that it's the same girl.

It's a neat idea for a plot—a bit like *A Slight Ache*, perhaps, in being rather too patterned, and once again you only have to scratch the nice girl to find the tart underneath. Sally is made to behave so differently with the aunts from the way she behaves in the club that she's hardly the same person. But a lot of the dialogue is very good, and Pinter has a great deal of fun on the way with names (Milly, Sally, Wally, Tully), and with rhymes (Lascar from Madagascar). What is more important, though, is that he's developing the technique of the bravura boasting fantasy, putting in some very bizarre touches that look forward to both Harry and Bill in *The Collection* and to Lenny in *The Homecoming*. Walter's fantasies are very much more elaborate than Albert's lies to the tart in *A Night Out* about being an assistant director in films.

> WALTER: Ever met a gunman before?
>
> SALLY: I don't think so.
>
> WALTER: It's not a bad life, all things considered. Plenty of time off. You know, holidays with pay, you could say. No there's plenty of worse occupations. You're not frightened of me now you know I'm a gunman, are you?
>
> SALLY: No, I think you're charming.
>
> WALTER: Oh, you're right there. That's why I got on so well in prison, you see. Charm. You know what I was doing in there, I was running the prison library. I was the best librarian they ever had. The day I left the Governor gave me a personal send off. Saw me all the way to the gate. He told me busi-

ness at the library had shot up out of all
recognition since I'd been in charge.

SALLY: What a wonderful compliment.

WALTER (*pouring more drink*): He told me
that if I'd consider giving up armed robbery
he'd recommend me for a job in the British
Museum. Looking after rare manuscripts.
You know, writing my opinion of them.

SALLY: I should think that's quite a skilled job.

WALTER: Cheers. Skilled? Well, funny enough,
I've had a good bit to do with rare manuscripts in my time. I used to know a bloke
who ran a business digging them up.

SALLY: Digging what up?

WALTER: Rare manuscripts. Out of tombs. I
used to give him a helping hand when I was
on the loose. Very well paid it was too. You
see, they were nearly always attached to a
corpse, these manuscripts, you had to lift up
the pelvis bone with a pair of tweezers. Big
tweezers. Can't leave finger-prints on a
corpse, you see. Canon law. The biggest
shock I ever had was when a skeleton col-
lapsed on top of me and nearly bit my ear off.
I had a funny feeling at that moment. I
thought I was the skeleton and he was my
long lost uncle come to kiss me goodnight.
You've never been inside a grave, I suppose.
I can recommend it, honest, I mean if you
want to taste everything life has to offer.

Solto, the landlord, is a kind of Goldberg, but he
makes less impact and isn't so funny. He talks at
length about himself in much the same way, with
Jewish rhythms clearly discernible in his speech. He
also repeats the Goldberg pattern of wooing the girl

away from the young man (towards whom he pretends to be well-disposed) and taking her for himself.

While the night club dialogue is typical of Pinter, with its repetitiveness and its definite rhythm, it's also reminiscent of T. S. Eliot.

> TULLY: . . . Don't you remember me at Blackheath.
> SOLTO: You're going back a bit.
> TULLY: I'm going back a few years before the war.
> SOLTO: You're going back to when the game was good.
> TULLY: What about you at Blackheath?
> SOLTO: Blackheath. It's another story when you start talking about Blackheath.

Perhaps Pinter owes more to T. S. Eliot than has been recognized, as the following excerpt from *Sweeney Agonistes* shows.

> DUSTY: How about Pereira?
> DORIS: What about Pereira?
> I don't care.
> DUSTY: You don't care!
> Who pays the rent?
> DORIS: Yes he pays the rent.
> DUSTY: Well some men don't and some men do.
> Some men don't and you know who.
> DORIS: You can have Pereira.

The Dwarfs

The Dwarfs, which was staged at the Arts in December 1960, is hardly a play at all. Taken from Pinter's unpublished novel of the same name, it's a completely unstructured series of fragmentary and often incoherent conversations between three friends: Len, Pete, and Mark. The main interest of the piece is that it shows us in their crudest form some of the themes which Pinter developed in the plays.

It starts off with a scene in which Len and Pete are eating and drinking in Mark's room, complaining, like the gunmen in *The Dumb Waiter*, that so little has been prepared for them. A lot of the dialogue is schizophrenic, and not put into sufficient perspective by Pete's telling Len that he's heading for the looney bin, or by Len's telling Pete that he's a nut. Often the rhythm is so strong that it verges on verse, and one of Len's speeches is laid out like verse. Again language and some of the cadences make us think of T. S. Eliot.

MARK: What do you think of it?

LEN: It's not a schmutta.

MARK: It's got a zip at the hips.

LEN: A zip at the hips? What for?

MARK: Instead of a buckle. It's neat.

LEN: Neat? I should say it's neat.

MARK: No turn-ups.

LEN: I can see that. Why didn't you have turn-ups?

MARK: It's smarter without turn-ups.

LEN: Of course it's smarter without turn-ups.

MARK: I didn't want it double-breasted.

LEN: Double-breasted? Of course you couldn't have it double-breasted.

MARK: What do you think of the cloth?

LEN: The cloth? (*He examines it, gasps and whistles through his teeth. At a great pace.*) What a piece of cloth. What a piece of cloth. What a piece of *cloth.*

MARK: You like the cloth?

LEN: WHAT A PIECE OF CLOTH!

(It may also have been T. S. Eliot who infected Pinter with the delight he takes in the names of London districts.)

The action moves from Mark's room to Len's room, and for Len, his room isn't the safe and stable place that a room usually is.

The rooms we live in . . . open and shut. (*Pause.*) Can't you see? They change shape at their own will. I wouldn't grumble if only they would keep to some consistency. But they don't. And I can't tell the limits, the boundaries, which I've been led to believe are natural. I'm all for the natural behaviour of rooms, doors, staircases, the lot. But I can't rely on them.

Pete has one very explicit speech which starts off rather like a speech of Teddy's in *The Homecoming*.

> The apprehension of experience must obviously be dependent upon discrimination if it's to be considered valuable. That's what you lack. You've got no idea how to preserve a distance between what you smell and what you think about it. You haven't got the faculty for making a simple distinction between one thing and another.

But it veers off into a description of a dream of being trapped on a platform in a subway station and seeing people's faces disintegrating, lumps of flesh falling off. The image of the mirror and the fear of losing identity are recurrent motifs, and there seems to be a connection between these and the image of the scavenger dwarfs of the title, who seem to feed on people, as Pete and Len were trying to feed off Mark's supplies in his absence. But none of this is at all clear. We are told that the dwarfs only work in cities, and the way Len speaks of their being "on the job" makes us associate them with Goldberg and McCann, or Gus and Ben.

The script becomes more and more incoherent as it goes on. Len feels used, persecuted by the other two, talks of the hole they have made in his side, which he cannot plug. The writing becomes surreal, Joycean, mad, and the madness is blamed on to the food. Len says he's eaten too much stale cheese—"It got me in the end"—and then suddenly the language becomes very clear again as Len makes an explicit statement about the nature of identity.

The point is, who are you? Not why or how, not even what. I can see what, perhaps, clearly enough. But who are you? It's no use saying you know who you are just because you tell me you can fit your particular key into a particular slot which will only receive your particular key because that's not foolproof and certainly not conclusive. Just because you're inclined to make these statements of faith has nothing to do with me. It's not my business. Occasionally I believe I perceive a little of what you are but that's pure accident. Pure accident on both our parts, the perceived and the perceiver. It's nothing like an accident, it's deliberate, it's a joint pretence. We depend on these accidents, on these contrived accidents, to continue. It's not important then that it's conspiracy or hallucination. What you are, or appear to be to me, or appear to be to you, changes so quickly, so horrifyingly, I certainly can't keep up with it and I'm damn sure you can't either. But who you are I can't even begin to recognize, and sometimes I recognize it so wholly, so forcibly, I can't look, and how can I be certain of what I see? You have no number. Where am I to look, where am I to look, what is there to locate, so as to have some surety, to have some rest from this whole bloody racket? You're the sum of so many reflections. How many reflections? Whose reflections? Is that what you consist of? What scum does the tide leave? What happens to the scum? When does it happen? I've seen what happens. But I can't speak when I see it. I can only point a finger. I can't even do that. The scum is broken and sucked back. I don't see where it goes, I don't see when, what do I see, what have I

seen? What have I seen, the scum or the es-
sence? What about it? Does all this give you the
right to stand there and tell me you know who
you are? It's a bloody impertinence.

The Collection

The Collection was first seen on television in May 1961 and staged at the Aldwych in June 1962, jointly directed by Peter Hall and Harold Pinter. It is written in short scenes which are extremely well put together, and its dialogue is full of thrust and bite, though the stage production did not make the impact it could have made, in spite of a nicely judged performance from Michael Hordern as Harry.

Compared with the rest of Pinter's later work, *The Collection* is remarkable for its economy. There is no padding and all the details count. The fruit juice, the olives and Stella's kitten all contribute, not to the plot but to the characterization and atmosphere, which are built up subtly, without explicitness.

As usual in Pinter, we learn next to nothing about the surrounding circumstances. All four characters are involved in the dress business, but Pinter only mentions this in passing. And of course we learn nothing about motivation. Why is James so intent on making some kind of personal contact with Bill? What does Stella feel towards each of the three men? The four characters are linked together by emotional interdependencies, but there is no question of sorting out the tangle of crossed lines. What Pinter gives us has to be enough and, in its curious way, it is.

The play stands up as a satisfying whole, even though we are given so few facts, and even though so much of what the characters themselves say may be fiction. Perhaps Harry's story about picking Bill up in an East End slum is true. Perhaps it's a distortion of the truth. Perhaps it's a complete fiction. Where Pinter succeeds so well is in establishing a convention and a frame of plot development in which the unanswered questions don't distract us from looking at what he wants to show us—or prevent us from being satisfied with what he gives us. The value of the incident in Leeds, whatever it was, is that its consequences illuminate all the insecurities that the characters have about themselves and each other. Harry doesn't trust Bill, James doesn't trust Stella, and neither Bill nor Stella, obviously, are finding fulfilment in their lives with their partners. Without sketching in any of the past history of these relationships, or even developing them very much in the present tense, Pinter draws on the insecurities to build up a most effective tension.

This time we have two rooms and two couples, with one member of each couple as a threat to the peace of the other couple. The play starts very much like a conventional thriller with a dim figure inside a telephone box at four o'clock in the morning. Inside Harry's house, the ringing of the telephone announces the menace from outside. We then find from the way he talks to Harry that Bill is apprehensive about meeting the stranger who is so persistent in trying to contact him. But once the two men meet, although the tension survives, the tenor of the conversation is very different from that of the conventional husband talking to the man he suspects of having slept with his wife.

> JAMES: Got any olives?
> BILL: How did you know my name?
> JAMES: No olives?
> BILL: Olives? I'm afraid not.
> JAMES: You mean to say you don't keep olives for your guests?
> BILL: You're not my guest, you're an intruder. What can I do for you?
> JAMES: Do you mind if I sit down?
> BILL: Yes, I do.
> JAMES: You'll get over it.
>> *(James sits. Bill stands. James stands, takes off his overcoat, throws it on an armchair, and sits again.)*
> BILL: What's your name, old boy?
>> *(James reaches to a bowl of fruit and breaks off a grape, which he eats.)*
> JAMES: Where shall I put the pips?
> BILL: In your wallet.
>> *(James takes out his wallet and deposits the pips.)*

The conversation which follows contains some good examples of Pinter's developing technique for suggesting tension beneath a surface of apparent relaxation. And once again, as in *Night School*, Bill's outrageous boasts also point to his insecurity.

BILL: I'm expecting guests in a minute, you know. Cocktails, I'm standing for Parliament next season.

JAMES: Come here.

BILL: I'm going to be Minister for Home Affairs.

But quite apart from the comedy and the fantasy, the conversation is well developed on serious lines as the characters take up positions in relation to the mystery of what really happened. James speaks as if his wife has given him a full confession of how she met Bill in the elevator, how he went to her room in pyjamas and dressing gown, to ask for toothpaste, and how he refused to leave. As for us, we have no means of knowing whether his wife was telling the truth or whether he's telling Bill the truth about what his wife said to him. We know that Bill was in Leeds and we know that James knew Bill's name, but that's all. Bill's reactions are inconsistent, varying between amused dismissals of the charge and indications that he did sleep with the woman. But again we have no means of knowing whether or not the inconsistency is deliberate, contrived in order to tantalize James. The scene is something like the party scene in *The Birthday Party*: we have the hunter and the hunted; we have the conflict going on under the small talk as the characters drink; we have the mystery that adds to the menace—we don't know quite what it is all about. But the violence and the comedy are much more closely interwoven now.

BILL: . . . Ah well, it's been very nice meeting you, old chap. You must come again when the weather's better.

> *(James makes a sudden move forward.
> Bill starts back, and falls over a pouffe on
> to the floor. James chuckles. Pause.)*
>
> You've made me spill my drink. You've made
> me spill it on my cardigan.
> *(James stands over him.)*
> I could easily kick you from here.
> *(Pause.)*

Harry is the character who is least directly involved in the question, but he too is jealous and this
makes him behave just as erratically as the jealous
James or the evasive Bill. Pinter writes mad fantasy
speeches for him with elaborate casualness.

> BILL: I don't want any potatoes, thank you.
> HARRY: No potatoes? What an extraordinary
> thing. Yes, this chap, he was asking for you,
> he wanted you.
> BILL: What for?
> HARRY: He wanted to know if you ever cleaned
> your shoes with furniture polish.
> BILL: Really? How odd.
> HARRY: Not odd. Some kind of national survey.
> BILL: What did he look like?
> HARRY: Oh . . . lemon hair, nigger-brown
> teeth, wooden leg, bottle-green eyes and a
> toupee. Know him?

But in spite of the embroidery and the amusement,
the edge and the incisiveness of the dialogue are
never lost.

Back with Stella, James taunts her by appearing
to be debating with himself about whether or not to
do what we know he's done already—to go to see
Bill. When he finally admits that he's seen him, he

describes, comically, a dinner with him, which he probably never had. Or if he did have it, it wasn't at all like this. But again we're forced into playing the game of guessing how much of what he says is fiction.

> JAMES: . . . He entirely confirmed your story.
> STELLA: Did he?
> JAMES: Mmm. Only thing—he rather implied that you led him on. Typical masculine thing to say, of course.
> STELLA: That's a lie.
> JAMES: You know what men are. I reminded him that you'd resisted, and you'd hated the whole thing, but that you'd been—how can we say—somehow hypnotized by him, it happens sometimes. He agreed it can happen sometimes. He told me he'd been hypnotized once by a cat. Wouldn't go into any more details, though. Still, I must admit we rather hit it off. We've got the same interests. He was most amusing over the brandy.

By now we are involved in such a complex calculus of distortion that we are quite contented to lose sight of the basic question of whether Bill has slept with Stella, which must be answerable with a simple yes or no.

Stella is the least satisfactory character. Pinter allows her no humor and no fantasy. Put under pressure, all she can do is burst into tears, and James's long speech about Bill is implicitly a criticism of the limitations of their marriage. It reminds us of Mick in *The Caretaker* talking down to Davies about the people he knows, making them sound far more interesting than the person he's talking to.

He's a very cultivated bloke, your bloke, quite a considerable intelligence at work there, I thought. He's got a collection of Chinese pots stuck on a wall, must have cost at least fifteen hundred a piece. Well, you can't help noticing that sort of thing. I mean, you couldn't say he wasn't a man of taste. He's brimming over with it. Well, I suppose he must have struck you the same way. No, really, I think I should thank you, rather than anything else. After two years of marriage it looks as though, by accident, you've opened up a whole new world for me.

At the end, the conflict is resolved and the pattern completed very neatly, without of course answering the basic question. Harry repeats James's telephone trick by ringing up Stella and not saying who he is. There's a very Pinteresque scene in which violence seems to be pending and James throws a knife at Bill, who cuts his hand in catching it. But the fact that Harry is standing in the doorway reduces the tension in one way to heighten it in another. It is Harry who finally takes charge of the situation by telling James that Stella has confessed to him that the whole story was made up. But, as before, we know neither whether Stella told Harry the truth nor whether Harry is telling Bill and James the truth about what Stella told him.

In any case the important part of the scene isn't what Harry says about Stella but what he says about Bill. He is given good, terse, humorous, cutting lines all through the scene, culminating in a long speech with many reiterations of the word "slum."

Bill's a slum boy, you see, he's got a slum sense of humour. That's why I never take him along with me to parties. Because he's got a slum mind. I have nothing against slum minds *per se*, you understand, nothing at all. There's a certain kind of slum mind which is perfectly all right in a slum, but when this kind of slum mind gets out of the slum it sometimes persists, you see, it rots everything. That's what Bill is. There's something faintly putrid about him, don't you find? Like a slug. There's nothing wrong with slugs in their place, but he's a slum slug; there's nothing wrong with slum slugs in their place, but this one won't keep his place—he crawls all over the walls of nice houses, leaving slime, don't you, boy? He confirms stupid sordid little stories just to amuse himself, while everyone else has to run round in circles to get to the root of the matter and smooth the whole thing out. All he can do is sit and suck his bloody hand and decompose like the filthy putrid slum slug he is.

After this, Bill tells James what he says is the real truth—that he sat in the lounge with Stella for two hours, talking about what they would do together if they went up to her room, but never going. James seems to accept this as the truth, since he goes home and confronts Stella with it. She neither confirms nor denies it, and of course Pinter is quite right not to let her.

The Lover

The Lover, which was televised in March
1963 and staged six months later, received more pub-
licity than The Collection, but it is not as good a play.
It is thinner in texture and the idea is dragged out to
greater length than it really warrants. It has certain
resemblances to The Collection. The game that Richard and Sarah play with each other by pretending
that they are being unfaithful to each other in the
afternoon (Sarah's afternoon lover is actually Richard
in different clothes) isn't altogether unlike the games
played by the characters in The Collection, who tell
each other lies about the alleged infidelity. And in
both cases, part of the tension for us is the game that
Pinter's playing in making us try to sort out the fiction
from the facts. In both plays, the game has an unpleasant side to it, and the characters work up a good
deal of real anger about infidelities which may be
imaginary, but the anger illuminates characteristics
which wouldn't otherwise have been seen.

As in *The Collection*, we find out very little about the surrounding circumstances. Where Richard's money comes from, whether he really has an office, what he does and where he changes his clothes all remain mysteries. We know nothing about him except the way he talks and behaves in the two roles that he has chosen for himself. As in *The Collection*, the woman's character is less explored than the man's. Sarah varies between yielding and resisting, but it's always Richard who takes the initiative, and it is he who finally gets bored with the game and starts to break its rules, dragging the apparatus of the afternoon (the bongo drums) into the evening and forbidding Stella to go on receiving her lover.

But it is in the development of this change in Richard that we see that the writing is less successful than in *The Collection*. With all the questions that the earlier play left unanswered, we never felt that we wanted more information than it was giving us, and however obscure the characters' motives remained, we never felt that we needed to know more about them. Here, however, it is difficult to accept Richard's change of attitude as necessary to him. It is necessary to the script as being a twist to take the situation further, but as a development of the character as established, it seems contrived.

Again as in *The Collection*, there's a great deal of charm in the writing, particularly in the affectation of smiling casualness when the matters being discussed would normally make tempers rise.

> RICHARD (*amiably*): Is your lover coming today?
> SARAH: Mmnn.

RICHARD: What time?

SARAH: Three.

RICHARD: Will you be going out . . . or staying in?

SARAH: Oh . . . I think we'll stay in.

RICHARD: I thought you wanted to go to that exhibition.

SARAH: I did, yes . . . but I think I'd prefer to stay in with him today.

RICHARD: Mmn-hmmn. Well, I must be off.

But the development of the situation lacks the economy we have come to expect of Pinter, and as they go on talking to each other about their lovers in several different scenes, separated by fades and quick costume changes, nothing very much is added. A superfluous scene with the milkman has to be written in to give Richard time to change his clothes in order to be Max the lover.*

The silent scene with the bongo drums was more effective on television, where the director, Joan Kemp-Welch, showed us their fingers in close-up, first scratching at each other and at the drum. The excitement builds up until his fingers pounced on her fingers like a tarantula, and her hand frantically tries to escape, flailing at the drum. And then, after this sexy prologue to it, they play their first game. Richard first pretends to be Max pretending to be a stranger accosting her in a park, and later he pretends to be the kindly park employee who rescues her and takes her into his hut.

---

* When the play was televised, the critic of one of the daily papers thought it was a false economy to let one actor play the two parts.

This scene is very good up to the point where he says "It's teatime, Mary," and they both disappear under the tablecloth together; but in the ensuing conversation, Richard (in his role as the lover) discusses with Sarah the attitude of her husband to the knowledge that his wife has a lover. This is too much like the preceding conversation before we knew that he was the lover and that he was discussing exactly the same question in his role as the husband. The tension increases slightly when Richard makes Max threaten to get together with Richard (just like James's threat to Stella in *The Collection*) and to end the affair. Sarah is displeased at his departure from the normal routine.

> I want to whisper something to you. Listen. Let me whisper to you. Mmmm? Can I? Please? It's whispering time. Earlier it was teatime, wasn't it? Wasn't it? Now it's whispering time.
> *(Pause.)*
> You like me to whisper to you. You like me to love you, whispering. Listen. You mustn't worry about . . . wives, husbands, things like that. It's silly. It's really silly. It's you, you now, here, here with me, here together, that's what it is, isn't it? You whisper to me, you take tea with me, you do that, don't you, that's what we are, that's us, love me.

Vivien Merchant, with her warm whispers, was at her memorably sexy best in this speech.

This is the first Pinter play in which there has been no violence. All we get are conflicts of will, as in Richard's attempt to abolish the game, to merge the two parts he plays into one and the afternoons into the evenings. At first Sarah hates it when he uses phrases as Richard which he is only entitled to use as Max, when he pulls the hidden bongo drums from the cupboard, and when he goes into the park employee game and crawls to her under the table. But the ending is typically ambiguous. He seduces her into joining in the game with him and succeeds in making the two roles into one, but instead of throwing out the infidelity-in-the-afternoon fantasy, this seems just to be letting it encroach into the evenings. The ambiguity is a delicate and suitable one, and this play could not have taken us any further anyway.

Tea Party

The main weakness of the TV drama *Tea Party* is that it does not seem to be working towards any kind of statement. Pinter's plays usually do make a statement, even when it's one that couldn't be translated into any other words than those Pinter himself has used, as in *The Birthday Party*. The same is true when the play is built precariously over a manhole of doubt, as in *The Collection*, or when the statement is highly ambiguous, as at the end of *The Lover*. But in *Tea Party*, for the first time, the mystifications seem to be there for their own sake. We are constantly titillated by the hints that something is going to be unraveled, the implicit promise of a resolution which never comes. In *The Collection*, we don't need to know any more than we are told about the relationship between Harry and Bill, because nothing relevant hinges on it. In *Tea Party*, however, we do need to know more than we're told about the relationships between Disson and Wendy, his secre-

tary, Diana, his wife, and Willy, her brother, because
that's what the play is about, or seems to be.

As in *A Slight Ache*—which it also resembles in
the way it presents "affluence"—the hints of symboli-
cally failing sight are confusing. The optician repeat-
edly tells Disson that there's nothing wrong with his
eyes, while he himself is increasingly bothered by
them and so are we, through the tricks that are played
on us with the television cameras. When he's playing
ping-pong with Willy, we suddenly see two balls
bouncing towards him, and us. When one of his
young sons is holding the wood for him to saw, the
saw seems to be going right through the boy's fingers.
And again we are forced into identifying with his
failing eyesight when the television screen goes black
and the dialogue goes on.

> WENDY: I'm here, Mr. Disson.
> DISSON: Where?
> WENDY: You're looking at me, Mr. Disson.
> DISSON: You mean my eyes are open?

These are effective and frightening moments, but
wilfully cryptic. There's obviously some connection
between Disson's troubles with his eyes and the fact
that he's only attractive to Wendy when he lets her
blindfold him with her chiffon.

> Don't you like my chiffon any more, to put
> round your eyes? My lovely chiffon?
> *(Pause. He sits still.)*
> I always feel like kissing you when you've got
> that on round your eyes. Do you know that?
> Because you're all in the dark.
> *(Pause.)*
> Put it on.

(She picks up the chiffon and folds it.)
I'll put it on . . . for you. Very gently.
(She leans forward. He touches her.)
No—you mustn't touch me, if you're not
wearing your chiffon.

This was a very good moment for Vivien Merchant, whose voice was as seductive as in the "whispering time" speech in *The Lover*, but the hint that the
man is only attractive to the woman if he acquiesces in
being blind is neither developed nor integrated into
the texture of the play. Our understanding of what is
going on is blurred still further by the suggestion that
Disson's other senses may be failing too. One of the
most confusing moments of all comes when we are
told that Diana has gone home and we know that
Wendy is in the next-door room with Willy. We hear
laughter, as if they are flirting together, then just
after Disson has knelt down to peer through the key-
hole, Diana opens the door. Tricks like this have their
effect, but it is both cheap and confusing.

If the play contains any statements at all, it seems
to be making them about marriage, but making them
in a highly personal way, without wanting to communicate them to us. Marriage is certainly the main
motif. After the opening interview with Wendy, who
says she left her last job because her chief never
stopped touching her, Disson announces that he is
getting married tomorrow morning, and the next two
scenes are focused on the decision that Willy shall re-
place the best man, who is ill. At the reception after
the ceremony, Willy, whose relationship with his sister is highly ambiguous, proposes a toast in honor of
the groom by talking almost entirely about the bride.

Tea Party is like *The Collection* in the alignment of the four main characters. This time they are not divided clearly into two couples, with one of each becoming a threat to the peace of the other, but when Diana becomes Willy's secretary, we get a criss-crossing of dependencies and loyalties, and personal insecurity figures a great deal in the tensions and conflicts which develop. But whereas, in *The Collection*, each character was clearly in focus (except perhaps Stella), here Wendy, Diana, and Willy are all mysteriously out of focus, while the focus on Disson, who is put squarely in the center of the picture, is deliberately blurred by the way we are made to identify with his blurred vision. And as usual, we are given no insight into his motivations, which seem highly erratic. When he has most reason to be suspicious of Willy, he acts most generously towards him, making gestures which are going to involve him more and more deeply with the man. After Willy's speech at the reception, which is implicitly so insulting to Disson, he offers him a job in the firm, and it is when he is angry with him for whispering with Diana that he offers him a partnership. His intention may be to bribe Willy and his motivation may be anxiety. This could be a good point if it became clearer, but it is only seen in the same confused perspective as everything else.

The ending is the most confused and confusing of all. It is reminiscent of *The Birthday Party*. The blindfolding of Disson harks back to the game of blindman's buff, and the culmination of the whole play is the reduction of Disson to helpless passivity. But in *The Birthday Party*, the demolition of Stanley had a kind of rightness about it: it was a continuation in external terms of a tendency that had started inside Stanley, so that the choice of him as a victim was not entirely arbitrary. Disson, however, would never choose himself as a victim or see himself as a failure. No doubt there would be levels in such a man on which he does do both, but the play doesn't concern itself with exploring or explaining them.

The scene of the tea party is quite effective, with Disson ill and blind, isolated in a chair while the other guests eat and talk and enjoy themselves at his expense. But there is a puzzling scene in which Willy gets Diana and Wendy to lie down on Wendy's desk. From the expression on their faces, he seems to be making love to them, but the television cameras were cheating by cutting out the full picture of whatever was going on and giving us only a close-up of their faces.

Willy, Wendy, and Diana are now a mysterious triangle, while all the other characters are in pairs: the two old ladies at the buffet table, Disson's parents, the optician and his wife, and Disson's twin sons. Only Disson himself is on his own, with his eyes bandaged. Willy's persecution of him culminates in putting a ping-pong ball into his hand, which clutches it. The enigmatic end comes when a shoe drops to the floor at the base of Wendy's desk. We still have no idea of what has been happening on top of the desk. At this, Disson falls to the floor in his chair, and everybody has great difficulty in getting him up. They try and fail to get him out of the chair. The last word is Diana's:

> Can you hear me?
> *(Pause.)*

Robert, can you see me?
(Pause.)
It's me. It's me, darling.
(Slight pause.)
It's your wife.
(Close up Disson's eyes. Open.)

The Homecoming

In Pinter's second full-length play, *The Homecoming*, the subject is once again home. But this time the danger is inside and the victim comes from outside. The occupants are more aggressive and destructive than ever before (an ex-butcher, a pimp, and a demolition worker who wants to go professional as a boxer), and the victim is an outsider who was at one time an insider. A member of the family who left home, he now suffers by losing his wife when he brings her on a visit to the all-male ménage. The fear of losing a woman has been thematic in earlier plays, though less explicitly. The blind Negro in *The Room* is a threat to Bert's ownership of Rose with his luring line "Come home, Sal." Stanley in *The Birthday Party* and Wally in *A Night Out* would probably have never made it with their girls anyway, but in so far as they lose them, it is to an older man. James in *The Collection* derives pleasure as well as pain from the idea of Stella's infidelity with Bill, and Richard in *The Lover* has to invent an infidelity on the part of his wife. In *Tea Party*, Disson's hold over both Diana and Wendy is threatened by Willy, though Willy's relationships with the two women are never clarified.

In *The Homecoming*, once again the play opens with a one-sided conversation. The speaker is the father who has taken over the role of mother. Max's nagging, repetitive way of talking and Lenny's hostile indifference are established right from the start.

> MAX: What have you done with the scissors?
> *(Pause.)*
> I said I'm looking for the scissors. What have you done with them?
> *(Pause.)*
> Did you hear me? I want to cut something out of the paper.
> LENNY: I'm reading the paper.
> MAX: Not that paper. I haven't even read that paper. I'm talking about last Sunday's paper. I was just having a look at it in the kitchen.
> *(Pause.)*
> Do you hear what I'm saying? I'm talking to you! Where's the scissors?
> LENNY (*looking up, quietly*): Why don't you shut up, you daft prat?

Oblivious to the fact that he is being insulted and ignored, Max goes on reminiscing, filling in a good deal more plot background of past history than is usual in Pinter.

> I used to knock about with a man called Mac-Gregor. I called him Mac. You remember Mac? Eh? Huhh! We were two of the worst hated men in the West End of London. I tell you, I

still got the scars. We'd walk into a place, the whole room'd stand up, they'd make way to let us pass. You never heard such silence . . . He was very fond of your mother, Mac was. Very fond.

But the plotting is half-hearted and not very effective. The point of it is to establish a parallel between the mother (who was unfaithful to Max with Mac-Gregor) and Ruth, who is quite willing to be set up by the family as a whore. This may, for her, merely represent a return to the kind of life she led before marrying a philosophy teacher. If Teddy's mother was also a whore, as is suggested, Teddy's choice of wife would be understandable, but underneath Pinter's exaggeratedly casual treatment of the theme there is something compulsive about the equations he keeps drawing between the mother and the whore. As in *Tea Party*, he seems uncertain how far he wants the meaning the play has for him to be clear to other people.

Max is in some ways reminiscent of Goldberg, talking sometimes in the same rhythm but without the redeeming grain of humor in the writing, and without the fact of Jewishness ever being indicated by anything but the names of the characters—Max, Lenny, Sam, Joey, Teddy, Ruth.

Max is also reminiscent of Davies, particularly in the way he talks about missed opportunities in his past. The new element in the characterization is the rapid self-contradiction in talking about his dead wife.

> MAX: Mind you, she wasn't such a bad woman.
> Even though it made me sick just to look at

> her rotten stinking face, she wasn't such a
> bad bitch. I gave her the best bleeding years
> of my life, anyway.
>
> LENNY: Plug it, will you, you stupid sod, I'm
> trying to read the paper.
>
> MAX: Listen! I'll chop your spine off, you talk
> to me like that! You understand? Talking to
> your lousy filthy father like that!

Insults are thrown about like custard pies in the old
comedies, and Pinter writes them amusingly, never
repeating himself.

The 63-year-old Uncle Sam also reminds us of
Davies, with his self-important fantasies. He boasts
of being the best chauffeur in the firm, the one that
everybody asks for. The gentlest, weakest creature in
this menagerie of a ménage, he is the butt of incessant raillery from Max, just as Max is from Lenny, but
with the difference that Sam is a homosexual who has
been sexually frustrated all his life, which makes him
vulnerable to jokes about weddings.

> MAX: When you find the right girl, Sam, let
> your family know, don't forget, we'll give you
> a number one send-off, I promise you. You
> can bring her to live here, she can keep us all
> happy. We'd take it in turns to give her a
> walk round the park.
>
> SAM: I wouldn't bring her here.
>
> MAX: Sam, it's your decision. You're welcome
> to bring your bride here, to the place where
> you live, or on the other hand you can take a
> suite at the Dorchester. It's entirely up to
> you.

The dark hints of Max's sentence about giving her a
walk round the park—the threat that Max and the

family carry out against Teddy—again refer to the same recurrent motif, the fear of losing the woman.

With Lenny and Max we learn little about the surrounding circumstances of how they spend their lives; with Joey, the amateur boxer, and Sam, we learn perhaps too much—some of it is padding—but with Teddy and Ruth, when they arrive, we learn very little indeed. The dialogue is vague about what they are doing in England, where they have come from and how long they are staying. In addition, their behavior is erratic in a way quite different from that in which the family are erratic. Everything about the scene is improbable in a worrying way. Without having told anyone that they are coming, they arrive in the middle of the night and decide not to wake anyone up. At first Teddy tries to get Ruth to go to bed without him, saying that he wants to walk about for a few minutes. She then decides that she wants to go for a walk and goes without him, leaving him alone for his scene with Lenny, who comes in wearing pyjamas, explaining that he sleeps down here now. "Next door, I've got a kind of study, workroom-cum-bedroom next door now, you see." Saying nothing about Ruth or being married, Teddy goes upstairs at the end of the scene, and Ruth and Lenny have a scene which starts off without either of them knowing who the other is. It leads into a mad monologue from Lenny which is like something out of *The Dwarfs*.

> LENNY: You must be connected with my brother in some way. The one who's been abroad.
> RUTH: I'm his wife.
> LENNY: Eh listen, I wonder if you can advise

me. I've been having a bit of a rough time
with this clock. The tick's been keeping me
up. The trouble is that I'm not all that con-
vinced it was the clock. I mean there are lots
of things which tick in the night, don't you
find that? All sorts of objects, which, in the
day, you wouldn't call anything else but commonplace. They give you no trouble. But in
the night any given one of a number of them
is liable to start letting out a bit of a tick.
Whereas you look at these objects in the day
and they're just commonplace. They're as
quiet as mice during the daytime. So . . . all
things being equal . . . this question of me
saying it was the clock that woke me up,
well, that could very easily prove something
of a false hypothesis.

Like so many things in the play, this speech is
striking at the time but unexplained, arbitrary, and
structurally functionless. In the earlier Pinter, each
part had its place in the architecture of a whole, but
now, self-indulgent speeches like this are put in for
the sake of deliberate mystification and immediate
impact, irrespective of whether they contribute anything of value to the overall effect.

Lenny has a very long scene with Ruth and the
conversation is unbalanced all through. Pinter is usually very good at unbalanced conversations, but this
one doesn't work. After the clock speech,* Lenny

---

* Clocks often take on an unexpected importance in Pinter's plays. In A Night Out a clock is the weapon that
Albert first uses to threaten his mother and then to threaten
the tart. In The Caretaker, one of Davies's main grudges
against Aston is that he hasn't bought him a clock.

gives Ruth a glass of water which she hasn't asked for, inquires whether she minds his having one himself, interviews her about her holiday in Europe with Teddy, and asks whether she minds if he holds her hand. When she says "Why?", he answers "I'll tell you why," but goes off into a very long narrative about a night down by the docks when he met a woman who was falling apart with the pox and beat her up because she started taking liberties. Pinter doesn't allow Ruth to react to the surprising and irrelevant information except by taking on the role of interviewer: "How did you know she was diseased?" For a while they switch roles and he interviews her: 'You and my brother are newly-weds, are you?" but we soon get back to a second long monologue from Lenny about an old woman who asked him to help her shift an iron mangle from one room to another. It was too heavy for him, so he told her to stuff it up her arse and gave her a swift jab in the belly. This is rather reminiscent of Walter's attempt in *Night School* to impress Sally by pretending to be a criminal, but this time we do not know whether to believe the story.

The trouble is that until the sexual game they start playing with the glass of water, when Ruth suddenly says, "If you take the glass, I'll take you"—nothing except the question about handholding leads up to this—none of the conversation between Lenny and Ruth has anything to do with Lenny and Ruth. Not that Pinter's characters ever develop relationships with each other in the conventional way, but between Meg and Stanley, Davies and Aston, Bill and James, even Richard and Sarah, there is an interconnection in which the characters have a kind of consistency and a kind of freedom of choice. In *The Homecom-*

ing, Pinter is making his characters behave quite arbitrarily, with an arbitrariness that is his, not theirs.

In the family there is nothing but the common predatoriness to link Lenny, Max, and Joey together. Sam and Teddy are members of the family without having anything in common with it or with each other. Ruth is completely inscrutable both in relation to Teddy and to the family. Nobody's behavior seems to be affected by anyone else's behavior. In *Tea Party*, Disson's behavior towards Willy was often the opposite of what would have been expected. In *The Homecoming*, the relationship between action and reaction is not even one of opposites. Almost nothing seems to happen as a reaction to anything else that happens. Everyone's behavior consists of a series of unexpected, separate actions, each one either disconnected from the last or at a tangent with it, and the actions are separate, not only from each other, but from the personality of the protagonist. Harry in *The Collection* often behaved erratically but never lost his consistency. In *The Homecoming* only Teddy and Sam have any consistency at all, and in them it consists largely in the passivity with which they face the aggressions of their family. Lenny's only consistency is in his manner of speaking. Max hasn't even that amount of solidity, veering between animal mindlessness and a quite sophisticated badinage.

Quite apart from the implicit misanthropy, the undertone of the play is negative and pessimistic. In mood, it's rather like a *Troilus and Cressida* taken over entirely by Thersites and Pandarus.

> SAM: This is my house as well, you know. This was our mother's house.

MAX: One lot after the other. One mess after the other.

SAM: Our father's house.

MAX: Look what I'm lumbered with. One cast-iron bunch of crap after another. One flow of stinking pus after another.

(Pause.)

Our father, I remember him. Don't worry. You kid yourself. He used to come over to me and look down at me. My old man did. He'd bend right over me, then he'd pick me up. I was only that big. Then he'd dandle me. Give me the bottle. Wipe me clean. Give me a smile. Pat me on the bum. Pass me around, pass me from hand to hand. Toss me up in the air. Catch me coming down. I remember my father.

And Max's bitterness against his father is echoed by Lenny's against him.

I'll tell you what, Dad, since you're in the mood for a bit of a . . . chat, I'll ask you a question. It's a question I've been meaning to ask you for some time. That night . . . you know . . . the night you got me . . . that night with Mum, what was it like? Eh? When I was just a glint in your eye. What was it like? What was the background to it? I mean, I want to know the real facts about my background.

This unforgiving obsession with the moment of conception obviously stems from Beckett, whose characters adamantly refuse to forgive the "accursed progenitor" for the irreversible act of bringing them into the world. Max's final reaction to Lenny is to spit at him, which is the right reaction, because the question is entirely impersonal. Max and Lenny aren't even related to each other by genuine hostility. The characters in this play are more isolated from each other than in any other play by Pinter, but he does nothing to put the isolation into perspective.

Martin Esslin in his book *The Peopled Wound: The Work of Harold Pinter* explains the play in terms of the Oedipal theme. After the expulsion of a father figure by two sons in *The Caretaker*, after the rivalry with a father figure over a girl in *Night School*, and after *The Lover*, in which "the hero dreams of his wife (who is a mother) as a whore," Esslin says that it is in *The Homecoming* that the Oedipal theme emerges most fully and explicitly. "It is as though it had gradually risen to the surface as Pinter gained the self-confidence and formal skill that enabled him to meet it head on rather than merely obliquely." I would not have said that it was explicit in *The Homecoming* and it seems to me that where he treated it more obliquely, as in Stanley's relationship with Meg in *The Birthday Party*, the results were better. Although we are told that Ruth is a mother—like Jessie she has three children—this does not make her theatrically effective as a mother figure. She may be, as Esslin suggests, more like the dream mother of Lenny's and Joey's fantasies, still young and attractive, but the parallel between her and Jessie seems more verbally contrived than theatrically developed.

Even structurally, the climax of Act One is muffed. The scene in which Max bullies the pathetic Sam gets in the way of the long delayed confrontation between the married couple and the family. After so much rancor, so many squibs and thunderclaps of violence and threatened violence, we are so inured against the atmosphere of insults that it counts for very little when Max insults Ruth by calling her a tart. Whether he's right or not, whether she was one earlier or not is a question which in this perspective hasn't very much force. The actual violence, when it comes, comes, as we would by now expect, in an unexpected way. Max hits Joey in the stomach with all his strength and starts to collapse himself from the exertion of the blow. Sam goes to help him and for his pains gets hit on the head with Max's stick. The closing moment of the act is an equally enigmatic threat of tenderness between Max and Teddy as overloaded with menace as Ruth's threat of sex to Lenny.

> MAX: You want to kiss your old father? Want a cuddle with your old father?
> TEDDY: Come on, then.
>   *(They face each other.)*
>   Come on.
>   *(Pause.)*
> MAX: You still love your old Dad, eh?
>   *(They face each other.)*
> TEDDY: Come on, Dad. I'm ready for the cuddle.
>   *(Max begins to chuckle, gurgling. He turns to the family and addresses them.)*
> MAX: He still loves his father!

Act Two starts with the phoney conviviality of the family reunion. Again a Jewish tone can be heard in Max's speeches as he rejoices, not without irony, in his three fine grown-up lads, wishing his dead wife could be there to see them. The tone changes rapidly into bitchiness, and he plays the role of the wife nagging the husband to go out to work when he starts pitching into Sam, the unmasculine breadwinner. Then he gets back on his (and Pinter's) wedding hobbyhorse, talking now to Teddy:

> MAX: Did you have a big function?
> TEDDY: No, there was no one there.
> MAX: You're mad. I'd have given you a white wedding. We'd have had the cream of the cream here. I'd have been only too glad to bear the expense, my word of honour.
>> *(Pause.)*
> TEDDY: You were busy at the time. I didn't want to bother you.
> MAX: But you're my own flesh and blood. You're my first born. I'd have dropped everything.

One of the most effectively dramatic moments comes when Teddy, sensing that something is going to go wrong, tries to persuade Ruth to cut the visit short and go back with him to the States. But again Teddy's manner of handling Ruth is very odd indeed, without coming into focus as indicative in any way of his relationship with her.

> TEDDY: . . . Look, I just brought you back to meet the family, didn't I? You've met them, we can go. The fall semester will be starting soon.
> RUTH: You find it dirty here?
> TEDDY: I didn't say I found it dirty here.
>> *(Pause.)*
> I didn't say that.
>> *(Pause.)*
> Look. I'll go and pack. You rest for a while.

Will you? They won't be back for at least an
hour. You can sleep. Rest. Please.

(She looks at him.)

You can help me with my lectures when we
get back. I'd love that. I'd be so grateful for it,
really. We can bathe till October. You know
that. Here, there's nowhere to bathe, except the
swimming bath down the road. You know
what it's like? It's like a urinal. A filthy urinal!

Nobody realistically speaks to anybody else like that,
and the different kinds of departure from realism in
this play have not added up to any kind of convincing stylization.

After this, the play rapidly falls to pieces. There is
an unpleasant scene in which Joey and Lenny simul-
taneously embrace Ruth while Teddy and Max
watch, without interfering. The scene blacks out after
Teddy's speech about detachment, which I've quoted
already. There's an odd scene about a cheese roll of
Lenny's which Teddy has taken and eaten. It gen-
erates a kind of tension by its very oddness, but the
tension is quickly dissipated by Lenny's long homily
to Teddy. It is amusing that Lenny should protest so
strongly about losing his cheese roll when Teddy has
been silent about losing his wife, but the irony isn't
effective enough to sustain this speech for the length
Lenny takes it to, although it's a good monologue as
such. What is missing is overall coherence. In *The
Birthday Party*, we were made to care very much
about what was happening to Stanley, without understanding it. Here we neither understand nor care.

The play becomes still more gratuitously unpleasant when Joey comes downstairs after being in bed
with Ruth. He talks about it to Lenny and Teddy

joins in the conversation. What follows as the family arrange to set Ruth up as a tart is rather like Giles Cooper's *Everything in the Garden* without the humor and without the feeling of inevitability. What happened there was highly improbable but one step led insidiously and convincingly to the next, and although Giles Cooper allowed himself considerable comic license in representing the suburban types, they were incomparably more credible and more relevant to contemporary reality than Pinter's people. Even compared with his own early work, we miss the subtlety. In *The Birthday Party, The Room, The Dumb Waiter,* and *The Caretaker,* there was always an inevitability in the development. Here it seems contrived.

The end is the worst of all. Sam announces that MacGregor had Max's wife in the back of his cab while he was driving it and then collapses on the floor. Teddy goes and Max has some kind of attack.

> *(He falls to his knees, whimpers, begins to moan and sob. He stops sobbing, crawls past Sam's body round her chair, to the other side of her.)*
>
> I'm not an old man.
>
> *(He looks up at her.)*
>
> Do you hear me?
>
> *(He raises his face to her).*
>
> Kiss me.
>
> *(She continues to touch Joey's head, lightly. Lenny stands, watching.)*

The Basement

Originally conceived as a film, *The Basement* was made into a television play and broadcast in February 1967. It starts once again with a contrast between the warmth and safety of a room, where a man sits in an armchair reading a book, and the danger outside, where a man and a woman stand in the rain, hesitating before ringing the doorbell, like animals about to pounce on their prey. Law, the man inside, shows himself to be an easy victim. Lonely, he is glad to see Stott and hospitable to the extent of fussing.

> LAW: Here's a towel. Go on, give it a good wipe. That's it. You didn't walk here, did you? You're soaking. What happened to your car? You could have driven here. Why didn't you give me a ring? But how did you know my address? My God, it's years. If you'd have rung I would have picked you up. I would

have picked you up in my car. What happened to your car?

(Stott finishes drying hair, puts towel on chair arm.)

STOTT: I got rid of it.

LAW: But how are you? Are you well? You look well.

STOTT: How are you?

LAW: Oh, I'm well. Just a minute, I'll get you some slippers. *(Goes to cupboard, bends.)* You're going to stay the night, aren't you? You'll have to, look at the time. I wondered if you'd ever turn up again. Really. For years. Here you are. Here's some slippers.

(Stott takes slippers, changes shoes.)

I'll find some pyjamas in a minute. Still, we'll have a cup of coffee first, or some . . . Or a drink? What about a drink? You're not living at Chatsworth Road any more, are you? I know that. I've passed by there, numbers of times. You've moved. Where are you living now?

STOTT: I'm looking for a place.

When he invited Scott to stay for the night, Law did not know about the girl outside. Oddly, Stott has left her standing in the rain, which adds to the suspense and the mystery of how Law will be victimized, as he clearly will. The atmosphere of menace is unmistakable. As soon as Stott brings the girl in, she starts undressing and gets into Law's bed. The host watches with some consternation, but all he can say is "Can I get you some cocoa, some hot chocolate?" Stott gets into bed with her and starts to make love to her. Law picks up his book again.

The battle has begun. Stott—the name suggests

stoat—uses his ownership of the woman to fight for possession of the room. Law fights to regain the ascendancy in a series of almost ritualized contests of strength. This is Pinter's version of *The Games People Play*, and Law—true to what his name suggests—plays the competitive games according to the rules, which puts him at a disadvantage. When they agree to have a race in a muddy field, Stott wins by not running. Looking back to see what has happened to him, Law falls and gets covered with mud. He is also half-hearted in his fight for possession of the woman. He wants her, and, as we see in the geographically unexplained seaside scenes, she responds to him. In fact she betrays Stott by trying to persuade Law to throw him out of the apartment, but he turns down the chance of an alliance with her and betrays her betrayal to Stott, whom he still treats as a friend.

Both the aggression of the couple, who invade a man's house to make love in it, and the masochistic reaction of the victim are oddly close to what happens in Pinter's screenplay for the film *Accident*, based on Nicholas Mosley's novel. Coming back to his house after a visit to London, Stephen finds that Charlie and Anna have broken in to make love there. Stephen, who desires Anna, seems to be aware of the action as a kind of aggression and he is very angry; but we only hear the anger in the tone of voice he uses to stop Anna from making the bed. He tells her to leave it for the woman who comes in the mornings, but a moment later we see him making it himself. Then, going down the stairs with Charlie, he gives him a key of the house and invites him to use it for the weekend.

There is also a parallel between the games that are

played in the film and the games in *The Basement*. In both, aggressions are brought into a new kind of focus. In the tennis in the film, there is a kind of balance between the geniality on the surface and the violence which only sometimes breaks through, as if by accident, but the extraordinary game that the dinner-jacketed guests play with the cushion is openly violent. It is like a vicious form of Rugby in which people are aiming to hurt each other, and the dignity of the country house and the groomed glitter of the guests are invaluable as counterpoint. The scene makes a very valid point about the aggressive competitiveness inherent in this sort of sociality.

Although the purpose and the method of the two scripts often coincide, *The Basement* departs much further from naturalism than *Accident*. Pinter gives himself complete freedom to develop the conflict in any way that occurs to him, and in doing so, he exploits the medium to the full, using only a minimum of words in the dialogue but laying down in his stage directions detailed and astute instructions about the set, which virtually becomes a character in the play. After Law has been making love to Jane on the beach, he returns to the flat with her to find it unrecognizable. Stott is in possession of it and Scandinavian furniture has been installed. No one says anything about the change. Later, when the hostility of the two men is out in the open, they duel with broken milk bottles. Not only are they both stripped to the waist but the room too is suddenly bare. Pinter gives himself the same freedom in cutting between the room and the seashore without trying to indicate how much time elapses between one scene and the next, and summer changes casually into winter when only a second has gone by. But the method succeeds and the logic of the growing hostility working up through the games gives the action all the consistency it needs.

This freedom of movement in time and space represents a new departure for Pinter. In some ways, it is a development of the games played in *The Lover*, but here it is not just a matter of the characters playing a game. The whole play is a game in which one game creates the next. When Jane praises the room, Stott objects that it's too bright and starts turning off lights. When he makes love to Jane in the bed, Law's only reaction is to immerse himself in a Persian love manual, but in the first scene on the beach, which follows immediately, Law shows Jane that he knows more about Stott than she does.

> LAW: He has a connection with the French aristocracy. He was educated in France. Speaks French fluently, of course. Have you read his French translations?
>
> JANE: No.
>
> LAW: Ah. They're immaculate. Great distinction. Formidable scholar, Stott. Do you know what he achieved at Oxford? He achieved a First in Sanskrit at Oxford. A First in Sanskrit!
>
> JANE: How wonderful.
>
> LAW: You never knew?
>
> JANE: Never.
>
> LAW: I know for a fact he owns three châteaux. Three superb châteaux. Have you ever ridden in his Alvis? His Facel Vega? What an immaculate driver. Have you seen his yachts? Huh! What yachts. What yachts.

The writing here reminds us of the "true or false" game that Pinter has played with us so often, and the half-teasing tone is a bit like James's in *The Collection*, talking to Stella about Bill. Law is both hinting at a friendship between Stott and himself, from which Jane is excluded, and striking up a friendship with Jane, from which Stott is excluded. The next development is that from making love with Stott, Jane rolls over in the bed to smile at Law. Stott's next move in taking over the room is to take down all the pictures while Law looks on and agrees that they are terrible. This prepares the ground for the surprise of the complete change of décor in the apartment which is to come later. There is a pleasantly casual piece of one-upmanship from Stott in conversation with Law about Jane.

> STOTT: She comes from a rather splendid family, actually.
> LAW: Really?
> STOTT: Rather splendid.
> *(Pause.)*
> LAW: Very helpful, of course, around the house.
> STOTT: Plays the harp, you know.
> LAW: Well?
> STOTT: Remarkably well.
> LAW: What a pity I don't possess one. You don't possess a harp, do you?
> STOTT: Oh, yes. I've got a harp.
> LAW: A recent acquisition?
> STOTT: No, I've had it for years.

And of course Stott goes on making love to Jane in the bed after Law has started making love to her on the beach. In the restaurant scene, Stott scores a point by changing to Campari after Law has told the waiter that they all want the same again. And this is followed by the race scene. There is a winter scene in the yard—a circle of footprints in the snow, as if one prisoner has been exercising—with Law trying weakly to persuade Stott that the apartment is too small for three people, that the council would object, and so would the church. Stott walls the approach, and we see no release of aggression from Law until the summer scene in which he starts throwing phonograph records at the wall while looking for some Debussy which Stott wants. When he finds it and turns round with it in his hand, it is winter again and the room has reverted to its original furnishing.

After the whispering scene, when Law betrays Jane's betrayal to Stott, there is a scene rather reminiscent of Strindberg's *The Dance of Death*, with Stott apparently dying in bed and Jane and Law debating what to do with him. Then we see them in the corner "snuffling each other like animals," as Pinter's direction puts it. We never learn whether he was ill, or pretending, or why, but the next game is played with a recorder. Law irritates Stott deliberately by walking about the room, first playing it, then singing through it. Stott throws a bowl of fruit across the room and then, picking up a marble, prepares to bowl to Law, who readily responds by pretending to bat with the recorder. Stott barks the word "Play!" and as the sound crashes into the long silence, the marble crashes into the window. They go on playing, even after a marble hits Law in the face, drawing blood. Law wins the next point by batting a marble into the fishtank—water rushes out and we see a fish flapping about on the floor—but Stott knocks Law out with a final marble on the forehead. This is the last game before the duel with milk bottles, which reaches its climax in a close-up of the two jagged circles of glass crunching into each other. After this the starting positions are reversed. Stott is in possession of the room, which is furnished as at the beginning, and we see him in the armchair reading a book. Law is now in possession of Jane. We see them outside in the rain, preparing to ring. The closing words of the play are the same as the opening words, with the roles reversed and the characters reversed. Stott looks more like an easy victim; Law looks more dangerous.

It would have been impossible to contain all this within an hour of television without enormous economy and control. Visually it is richer and more varied than any of Pinter's other television plays, and although many of the scenes could only have been shot by prefilming, it exploits the possibilities of television to the full. Pinter's dialogue, always spare, is pared down to a minimum, but there is no mystification for the sake of keeping the audience guessing; what mystification there is serves the useful purpose of focusing our attention away from the surface of events and away from casual connections between them, onto the fears and anxieties and aggressions that are expressed in the actions and reactions, the playing and the fighting. We may start off by thinking "how odd" when Jane undresses, but soon we are following each move in the maneuvering for superiority as if we were watching a wrestling match, and the tension is all the greater for the fact that there are no rules in the game—or if Law thinks there are, then Stott knows that there is no penalty for breaking them.

Altogether the piece is rather like a Debussy prelude: the structure may appear to be arbitrary, but it is satisfying because it has a logic of its own.

Landscape

After *The Homecoming*, which was written in 1964, Pinter did not believe he would ever produce another full-length play. "My plays are getting shorter," he said in an interview printed in *The Times*, "words are so tender. One-act plays are all I seem to be able to write at the moment. I doubt if I will ever write something mammoth." In this he seemed to resemble Beckett who has not written a full-length play since *Happy Days* (1961).

Landscape lasts only thirty minutes. There are two characters, but there is no dialogue between them. We alternate between their two monologues. Duff talks of Beth* as "you" but most of the time he seems to be thinking of her rather than addressing her. She

---

* Vivien Merchant was playing Lady Macbeth at Stratford-on-Avon and Pinter was writing *Mac*—a memoir of the Irish actor-manager Anew MacMaster—but the joke about the missing "Mac" in the two names has no apparent bearing on anything in the text, and in any case neither name is ever mentioned.

talks about her man and an experience with him on a beach when she was naked under her beachrobe and whispered to him about having his child. But we are never altogether certain whether this man was Duff or someone else.

Landscape was written for the stage, but because the Lord Chamberlain objected to the word "fuck," and because Pinter refused to remove it, the play was premièred on the radio in April 1968. It was finally staged in July 1969, after the abolition of theatrical censorship*. But probably radio is the ideal medium for it, as it might have been for Beckett's *Play*, which is similar in keeping its characters immobile and having no physical action at all.

In *Play* all the action and in *Landscape* nearly all of it is set in the past. Pinter places his characters not in unlocalized urns but in the kitchen of a country house. His stage directions stipulate that "the background of a sink, stove, etc., is dim" and though Guy Vaesen's production started with an announcer's voice telling us where we were and that Beth was in an armchair and Duff in a chair at the table, the subsequent sound effects (introduced quite separately from the dialogue in well-defined pauses) seemed to generalize us away from the kitchen: gulls, a church bell, the lowing of cattle, a tractor, a plane, sparrows, a car. But all the sounds very faint. And though the house is important in their past— Duff and Beth were housekeeper and handyman to a Mr. Sykes but he's no longer there and recently they've had it to themselves—the dialogue which makes up the action (or the nondialogue which makes

---

* On a double bill with *Silence* at the Aldwych Theatre.

up the nonaction) could equally well be spoken anywhere. The characters are much more alive than in Beckett's *Play*—they have a present and a future as well as a past, they have desires, impulses, moods— but the action consists entirely of words and sounds.

The stage directions tell us that neither of them hears the other's voice and that Beth never looks at Duff, but the ambiguity about whether or not it is him she is talking about—like all the other ambiguities of their relationship—is served well by radio. With Peggy Ashcroft and Eric Porter in the parts, we were able to feel that speech was a convention by which they were both communicating their silent thoughts directly to us, not speaking out loud at all.

As in *Play*, the story is presented nonsequentially and impressionistically as flotsam from the relationship that the characters have shared washes up on the waves of present consciousness.

> DUFF: I was thinking . . . when you were young . . . you didn't laugh much. You were . . . grave.
> *(Silence.)*
> BETH: That's why he'd picked such a desolate place. So that I could draw in peace. I had my sketch book with me. I took it out. I took my drawing pencil out. But there was nothing to draw. Only the beach, the sea.
> *(Pause.)*
> Could have drawn him. He didn't want it. He laughed.
> *(Pause.)*
> I laughed, with him.
> *(Pause.)*
> I waited for him to laugh, then I would smile,

> turn away, he would touch my back, turn
> me, to him. My nose . . . creased. I would
> laugh with him, a little.
>> *(Pause.)*
> He laughed. I'm sure of it. So I didn't draw
> him.
>> DUFF: You were a first-rate house-keeper
>> when you were young. Weren't you? I was
>> very proud.

It also emphasizes the distance between them that
they live in such different mental climates. She talks
of snoozing in the sun, and sea and sand dunes. He
talks of walking the dog in the rain, puddles, pubs,
mud, shit.

He remembers a time when he was unfaithful to
her and told her about it afterwards. He also talks of
being proud of her and how the boss trusted her. But
primarily he talks of actions, things he has done and
things that have happened to him in the past, things
to be done in the future. She is less practical, more
self-involved, more of a dreamer. Her only allusion to
the future is to the time when she will no longer be
beautiful; but she is already in her late forties and
living in the past so much (in this empty house with
no master to make her do the housework) she seems
to think of herself as younger, more beautiful than
she is. She is apparently childless and this episode on
the beach, which could have led to childbirth, obses-
ses her. The deepest of the play's ironies is that the
ambiguity about the man becomes fairly unimportant.
Whether or not Duff was the man with her on the
beach, the man in her memory has nothing to do with
Duff as he is now. As with Stella in *The Collection,*
it matters very little whether she has made love to

another man or not. In either case the infidelity that Duff remembers pales to nothing by the side of the infidelity to him that is still going on. They have lived together for a long time but while he is—at least to some extent—still relating to her as she really is, either she has never related to him, or else stopped long ago. And there is a further irony in his enjoyment of the final abandonment of the attempt at communication.

> At least now . . . at least now, I can walk down to the pub in peace and up to the pond in peace, with no one to nag the shit out of me.

Even though the play may not fully communicate all these ironies to the listener who hears it only once, it succeeds immediately in establishing the contrasts between the two mental landscapes, between the preoccupations of the two characters. Both Beth and Duff use words very effectively to create their own personalities, defining themselves both by the words they choose and by the pictures they paint with them:

> DUFF: Do you remember the weather yesterday? That downfall?
> BETH: He felt my shadow. He looked up at me standing above him.
> DUFF: I should have had some bread with me. I could have fed the birds.
> BETH: Sand on his arms.
> DUFF: They were hopping about. Making a racket.
> BETH: I lay down by him, not touching.
> DUFF: There wasn't anyone else in the shelter.

There was a man and woman, under the trees, on the other side of the pond. I didn't feel like getting wet. I stayed where I was.

(Pause.)

Yes, I've forgotten something. The dog was with me.

(Pause.)

BETH: Did those women know me? I didn't remember their faces. I'd never seen their faces before. I'd never seen those women before. I'm certain of it. Why were they looking at me? There's nothing strange about me. There's nothing strange about the way I look. I look like anyone.

This total dependence on words is new for Pinter. Even in the three earlier plays which were written for radio (*A Slight Ache*, *A Night Out* and *Night School*) he relied more on action and less on the way the words hit the listener's ear. What is certain is that he could never have written *Landscape* had he not had so much experience of thinking in radio terms.

Silence

Silence was not planned as a sequel to Landscape. "It was one of those happy things that rarely happen with me," Pinter said in an interview quoted in The Times. "I always feel after completing something that I'll never write again, but then came Silence. It took a long time to write—longer in fact than any full-length play of mine."

Landscape and Silence together run less than two hours but this pleases Pinter. "I think evenings in the theatre tend to go on too long. I feel the audience will have quite enough with mine. They'll be glad to get out; they won't want any more . . ."

Landscape and Silence branch out quite a long way from the main trunk of Pinter's work. They make him seem rather like a symphonic composer turning to chamber music—Boulez-like music in which the intervals between the notes are almost more important than the notes themselves. Like Beckett in his later plays, Pinter is trying to draw not more but less

on the resources which the medium offers. *Landscape*
has no movement at all, *Silence* has only very little,
and the characters are less often talking to each other
than talking to themselves about themselves. They
have had and are still having relationships, but there
is no direct attempt to dramatize the relationships.
So there is no action, only the sketchiest suggestion of
plot, no violence and none of the atmosphere of
menace which was characteristic of all the plays from
The Room to *The Homecoming*.

Altogether the physical world becomes less important than the mental world in which the characters
live. The room is no longer a haven of apparent
safety from the dangers of the world outside or an
arena for a battle about territorial rights. Each of the
three characters in *Silence* has an area with a bed, a
table, and a chair in it. The stage direction makes no
mention of walls, and if there are walls they will not
be important as frontiers. The locale defined by the
designer no longer matters: the scenery is created by
the words. What Pinter is giving us now is a three-
dimensional poetry, a dialogue in which the words
do more of the work than ever before in his plays.

In *Silence* there are two men and a girl. Ellen is in
her twenties, Rumsey is forty, and Bates in his mid-
thirties. Rumsey's opening monologue, with its references to colors, weather, and movements, immediately creates a vivid impression of his mental world.

> I walk with my girl who wears a grey blouse
> when she walks and grey shoes and walks with
> me readily wearing her clothes considered for
> me. Her grey clothes.
> She holds my arm.

On good evenings we walk through the hills to
the top of the hill past the dogs the clouds racing just before dark or as dark is falling when
the moon.
When it's chilly I stop her and slip her raincoat
over her shoulders or rainy slip arms into the
arms, she twisting her arms.
And talk to her and tell her everything.
She dresses for my eyes.
I tell her my thoughts. Now I am ready to
walk, her arm in me her hand in me.
I tell her my life's thoughts, clouds racing. She
looks up at me or listens looking down. She
stops in midsentence, my sentence, to look up
at me. Sometimes her hand has slipped from
mine, her arm loosened, she walks slightly
apart, dog barks.

Ellen's monologue, which follows, also refers to
weather, to walking and to dogs. She is talking of the
men in her life.

There are two. One who is with me sometimes,
and another.
He listens to me. I tell him what I know. We
walk by the dogs. Sometimes the wind is so
high he does not hear me. I lead him to a tree,
clasp closely to him and whisper to him, wind
going, dogs stop, and he hears me.
But the other hears me.

Bates, the other man in her life, speaks in a rhythm
which contrasts with Rumsey's rhythm rather as
Duff's contrasts with Beth's in *Landscape*. The cadences are shorter, the manner rougher, brusquer.
The emphasis is on taking her, holding her, whereas

Rumsey was content to walk apart. And whereas Rumsey spoke of natural scenery, Bates talks of the town. The dog image here extends to the cars.

> Caught a bus to the town. Crowds. Lights round the market, rain and stinking. Showed her the bumping lights. Took her down around the dumps. Black roads and girders. She clutching me. This way the way I bring you. Pubs throw the doors smack into the night. Cars barking and the lights. She with me, clutching.
> Brought her into this place, my cousin runs it. Undressed her, placed my hand.

Rumsey seems less anxious to dominate Ellen, more patient, gentler and more willing to empathize with her.

> She walks from the door to the window to see the way she has come, to confirm that the house which grew nearer is the same one she stands in, that the path and the bushes are the same, that the gate is the same. When I stand beside her and smile at her, she looks at me and smiles.

> BATES: How many times standing clenched in the pissing dark waiting? The mud, the cows, the river.
> You cross the field out of darkness. You arrive.
> You stand breathing before me. You smile.
> I put my hands on your shoulders and press. Press the smile off your face.

Rumsey enjoys reading and watching the clouds. He likes silence. Bates resents noise but lives surrounded by it.

I'm at my last gasp with this unendurable racket. I kicked open the door and stood before them. Someone called me Grandad and told me to button it. It's they should button it. Were I young . . .

One of them told me I was lucky to be alive, that I would have to bear it in order to pay for being alive, in order to give thanks for being alive.

It's a question of sleep. I need something of it, or how can I remain alive, without any true rest, having no solace, no constant solace, not even any damn inconstant solace.

I am strong, but not as strong as the bastards in the other room, and their tittering bitches, and their music, and their love.

If I changed my life, perhaps, and lived deliberately at night, and slept in the day. But what exactly would I do? What can be meant by living in the dark?

For all three characters, the emphasis is on solitude. Ellen speaks about an elderly woman who tries to be friendly and quizzes her about her sexual experiences. But Ellen holds back from her.

I'm old, I tell her, my youth was somewhere else, anyway I don't remember. She does the talking anyway.

After all these monologues, Bates moves to Ellen and in a repetitious dialogue of very short lines tries, unsuccessfully, to persuade her to come out.

BATES: Come with me tonight.
ELLEN: Where?

> BATES: Anywhere. For a walk.
>   *(Pause.)*
> ELLEN: I don't want to walk.
> BATES: Why not?
>   *(Pause.)*
> ELLEN: I want to go somewhere else.
>   *(Pause.)*
> BATES: Where?
> ELLEN: I don't know.
>   *(Pause.)*
> BATES: What's wrong with a walk?
> ELLEN: I don't want to walk.

He goes on, puzzlingly, to talk to her about his cousin's place as if he had never mentioned it to her before. This throws doubt on his first monologue in which he said he took her there. Perhaps he was talking about another girl. Perhaps he was talking about Ellen but only imagined he took her. Perhaps he actually took her but is nevertheless talking as if he didn't expect her to remember the place. Perhaps the sequence in which we are watching events is not the sequence in which they happened. Just as the ambiguity focuses our attention on what is going on under the surface of events, so, with speech, Pinter is not mimicking or tape recording but listening for the movements that go on under the surface.

> BATES: I walk in my mind. But can't get out of the walls, into a wind. Meadows are walled, and lakes. The sky's a wall. Once I had a little girl. I took it for walks. I held it by its hand. It looked up at me and said, I see something in a tree, a shape, a shadow. It is leaning down. It is looking at us.

Maybe it's a bird, I said, a big bird, resting.
Birds grow tired, after they've flown over the
country, up and down in the wind, looking
down on all the sights, so sometimes, when
they reach a tree, with good solid branches,
they rest.

Poetry is used, like this, to draw in the contours on
the play's map of the character's mental scenery. But
this is not its only use. There is a short passage between Rumsey and Ellen in which the language,
partly by its rhythm, partly by its meaning, suggests
love-making.

> ELLEN: When I run . . . when I run . . . when
> I run . . . over the grass . . .
> RUMSEY: She floats . . . under me. Floating . . .
> under me.
> ELLEN: I turn. I turn. I wheel. I glide. I wheel.
> In stunning light. The horizon moves from
> the sun. I am crushed by the light.

But this suggestion of contact is immediately followed by a passage about noncontact, as if the whole
of life were lived on a parabola of nonmeeting.

> Sometimes I see people. They walk towards me,
> no, not so, walk in my direction, but never
> reaching me, turning left, or disappearing, and
> then reappearing, to disappear into the wood.
> So many ways to lose sight of them, then to re-
> capture sight of them. They are sharp at first
> sight . . . then smudged . . . then lost . . . then
> glimpsed again . . . then gone.

And further doubts about the nature of the contact
that exists between Rumsey and Ellen are raised by

the dialogue which follows, when she moves to his area. She notices that he has painted it and made shelves. The dialogue then makes the point that she has not been there since she was a little girl. There is also the suggestion of a little girl talking to a grown man in the way they speak to each other. As in her dialogue with Bates, the lines are kept very short.

> RUMSEY: Look at your reflection.
> ELLEN: Where?
> RUMSEY: In the window.
> ELLEN: It's very dark outside.
> RUMSEY: It's high up.
> ELLEN: Does it get darker the higher you get?
> RUMSEY: No.

As the play goes on, age seems to become more fluid and more metaphorical. Bates tells us of his landlady's asking him whether he is "nothing but a childish old man." Ellen asks herself whether she is old. Far removed though the play is from *The Room*, the characters' uncertainty about age seems to belong to the same order as Mr. Kidd's uncertainty about how many floors there are in the house. Essentially there is no way of measuring. You can only measure if you can relate and none of them can. They are all alone among other people, surrounded by silence which their speech does nothing to break. Ellen asks herself whether she is silent or speaking. When she goes to Rumsey and he advises her to find a young man, she first says that there aren't any, then that she doesn't like them. That she has been married is mentioned only to show how unimportant it is.

My drinking companion for the hundredth
time asked me if I'd ever been married. This
time I told her I had. Yes, I told her I had.
Certainly. I can remember the wedding.

Bates's little girl is similarly unimportant.

As the play approaches its end, the sections of
monologue become shorter, there are more reprises of
fragments from earlier dialogue and the juxtaposi-
tions become more pointed. *Silence* is neither like
one poem spoken by three voices nor like three
poems devised to intersect. It is like a totally new
kind of dramatic poem in which the relationships between the three kinds of poetry are clearer and more
important than the relationships between the three
characters on the level of action and physical contact.

Night

Night is a sketch which runs for seven minutes and took only forty minutes to write. "I was sitting with my wife after lunch. Normally I fall asleep, but on this occasion I suddenly got up, went upstairs and wrote *Night*. It came so easily."

It is less complex than *Silence* and closer in theme and form to *Landscape*, but comic. There is no movement, but it kept the audience at the Comedy Theatre in incessant fits of laughter.

A man and a woman in their forties are sitting at a table with their coffee. They are speaking to each other about memories of shared experience which come nowhere near to coinciding.

> MAN: We stopped and looked down at the river. It was night. There were lamps lit on the towpath. We were alone. We looked up the river. I put my hand on the small of your waist. Don't you remember? I put my hand under your coat.
> *(Pause.)*

WOMAN: Was it winter?

MAN: Of course it was winter. It was when we met. It was our first walk. You must remember that.

WOMAN: I remember walking. I remember walking with you.

MAN: The first time? Our first walk?

WOMAN: Yes, of course I remember that.
(Pause.)

WOMAN: We walked down a road into a field, through some railings. We walked to a corner of the field and then we stood by the railings.

MAN: No. It was on the bridge that we stopped.
(Pause.)

WOMAN: That was someone else.

As in *Landscape* and *Silence*, Pinter is no longer imitating colloquial speech. "There was no sound," the man says when the woman thinks she hears a child crying. "The house is silent." And as in *Landscape*, the barest outline of present circumstances is elaborately filled in with talk about the past. But through this talk, the essentials about the present relationship are created, very funnily, especially in the discussion about how he touched her.

MAN: I touched your breasts.

WOMAN: Where?

MAN: On the bridge. I felt your breasts.

WOMAN: Really?

MAN: Standing behind you.

WOMAN: I wondered whether you would, whether you wanted to, whether you would.

MAN: Yes.

WOMAN: I wondered how you would go about it, whether you wanted to, sufficiently.

MAN: I put my hands under your sweater, I undid your brassiere, I felt your breasts.

WOMAN: Another night perhaps. Another girl.

MAN: You don't remember my fingers on your skin?

WOMAN: Were they in your hands? My breasts? Fully in your hands?

MAN: You don't remember my hands on your skin?

(Pause.)

WOMAN: Standing behind me?

MAN: Yes.

WOMAN: But my back was against railings. I felt the railings . . . behind me. You were facing me. I was looking into your eyes. My coat was closed. It was cold.

MAN: I undid your coat.

WOMAN: It was very late. Chilly.

They are disagreeing less now, but significantly, it is just after he has mentioned that they walked down the towpath to a rubbish dump that she says he had her. He promised to adore her always and he says that he does. They had children, which are mentioned as casually as the child in *Silence*. The final emphasis is on her suspicion that his memories of her merge into his memories of other women and his suspicion that her memories of him merge into memories of other men. This comes in a passage in which they talk about their present conversation as if it were one of many in the past.

WOMAN: And we sat and talked and you remembered women on bridges and towpaths and rubbish dumps.

MAN: And you remembered your bottom against railings and men holding your hands and men looking into your eyes.

WOMAN: And talking to me softly.

MAN: And your soft voice. Talking to them softly at night.

WOMAN: And they said I will adore you always.

MAN: Saying I will adore you always.

Both of them seem quite content to digest their jealousy. Complacent about it, almost.

Old Times

In an interview for the radio recorded in September 1970, while he was still working on *Old Times*, Pinter described how he started it. "I was lying down on a sofa. I was reading a paper. And I did suddenly sit up, dashed upstairs. No reason at all. Nothing to do with what I was reading . . . And started to write. Two characters appeared on paper. I knew nothing about them. I've learned. I'm learning quite a bit about them . . . When I write I don't consider whether the characters are able to communicate or not able or in what way they're doing so or not doing so . . . I try to simply proceed from moment to moment between the characters and indeed the silences that fall between them . . . My job, as I see it, is really to shape an image on the stage. Let it live, but shape it in dramatic terms and leave it at that. I have nothing else to say. I'm only interested in the characters in that given situation."

It follows that the questions "What does it mean?"

and "What is the play about?" are equally liable to be dangerous, inviting a misleading translation of the images and the relationships into conceptual terms. A play like *Old Times* may give rise to a great many questions, philosophical and ontological questions, questions about time, memory and reality, but it is neither the play's purpose nor duty to suggest answers. The questions, rather, are part of a tremendously sophisticated game with the audience. For there are always two given situations: one between the characters, the other between the play and the audience. Pinter, of course, is by now very well aware of the attempts that will be made to impose meanings on each play he writes. He tries to remain immune to the pressure of audience expectations, and while he was writing *Old Times* he did not know whether it had any relation to any of his previous work. But there is no such thing as a nonrelationship with the audience you are writing for; in holding back from it—perhaps even to help himself to hold back from it—Pinter gently teases it. The characters also tease each other, and the two kinds of teasing overlap.

As the lights go up on Deeley and Kate in their converted farmhouse, a third figure, Anna, is in the background, dimly lit, looking out of the window. The other two, who are waiting for her, talk about her as if she is not there. But later, when she begins talking to Kate about the time, twenty years ago, when they were sharing an apartment and working as secretaries, it is clear that her move downstage (to join the others in the brighter light) is not meant to represent an entrance. She has heard them talking about the casserole that Kate has cooked.

> ANNA: You have a wonderful casserole.
>
> DEELEY: What?
>
> ANNA: I mean wife. So sorry. A wonderful wife.
>
> DEELEY: Ah.
>
> ANNA: I was referring to the casserole. I was referring to your wife's cooking.

Anna uses words like "lest" and "gaze," which, according to Deeley, are no longer used very often. Later, after he has described his first meeting with Kate in a cinema at a showing of *Odd Man Out* she says:

> There are some things one remembers even though they may never have happened. There are things I remember which may never have happened but as I recall them so they take place.

She goes on to describe how she once found Kate in the bedroom with a man who was sobbing, and later saw him on her bed, lying across her lap. She also talks about Sicily, where she says she is living, and about her husband. Abruptly, after a silence, she and Kate are discussing whether they should stay in or go out for the evening, talking to each other as if we had been transported back to the time when they were living together. But it is not a flashback because Deeley is able to interrupt and his line ("Hungry? After that casserole?") implies, on the contrary, a flash-forward to the time after dinner. As the act ends, he is the odd man out, for Anna, who is persuading Kate to stay in, is offering to invite a man over and suggesting various names, none of which are his. Kate will have a bath and decide, while doing so, which man should be asked over. Anna offers to run the bath for her but no, tonight she will run it for herself.

As the lights go up on Act Two we are still in the farmhouse but upstairs in the bedroom. Kate is in the bathroom, and Anna is sitting on one of the two divans. Deeley comes in with coffee and though the beginning of Act One implied that he had never met her, his first speech in Act Two ends "You prefer it white with sugar, I believe?" The suggestion that he has, in fact, met her before is developed almost immediately when he tells her he remembers her from a pub just off the Brompton Road and a party at someone's apartment in Westbourne Grove.

> DEELEY: You sat on a very low sofa, I sat opposite and looked up your skirt. Your black stockings were very black because your thighs were so white. . . . I simply sat sipping my light ale and gazed . . . gazed up your skirt. You didn't object, you found my gaze perfectly acceptable.

He also says he remembers seeing a girl friend of hers, who sat on the sofa with her at the party. After Kate reappears, fresh from her bath, Deeley refers again to *Odd Man Out*, comparing the smile on her face now with her smile when they walked down the street together after the film. Then Kate and Anna are again talking to each other as if they were still bachelor girls in London, discussing men and which one to invite round for the evening. And again Deeley interrupts, saying that one of them is out of town.

After a silence the conversation seems to switch back to the present place and the present time. In the play's opening conversation Kate said that Anna used to steal bits and pieces from her, including underwear. Now Anna says that once she borrowed some of Kate's underwear to go to a party and was punished for her sin when a man spent the whole evening looking up her skirt.

> ANNA: But from that night she insisted, from time to time, that I borrow her underwear— she had more of it than I, and a far greater range—and each time she proposed this she would blush, but propose it she did, nevertheless. And when there was anything to tell her, when I got back, anything of interest to tell her, I told her.

Deeley becomes very angry about the claim Anna is making to such an intimate share in his wife's past. "Sounds a perfect marriage," he sneers. Kate says very little but sides with Anna, telling her husband that if he doesn't like it he can go. Deeley's reprisal is to tell her about his earlier acquaintance with Anna, ironically using mock-hippy language.

> DEELEY: We had a scene together. She freaked out. She didn't have any bread, so I bought her a drink. She looked at me with big eyes, shy, all that bit. She was pretending to be you at the time. Did it pretty well. Wearing your underwear she was too, at the time. . . . She thought she was you, said little, so little. Maybe she was you. Maybe it was you, having coffee with me, saying little, so little.

Kate now, suddenly, talks as if she knew everything about Deeley's relationship with Anna, who found his face, she says, sensitive, vulnerable, and wanted to comfort it in the way only a woman can. Anna, who had at first denied having any memory of Deeley, now coolly admits to remembering him well, and Kate, in what seems like a final fusillade of quiet aggression, tells Anna that she remembers her dead.

> KATE: You didn't know I was watching you. I leaned over you. Your face was dirty. You lay dead, your face scrawled with dirt, all kinds of earnest inscriptions, but unblotted, so that they had run, all over your face, down to your throat. . . . When you woke my eyes were above you, staring down at you. You tried to do my little trick, one of my tricks you had borrowed, my little slow smile, my little slow shy smile, my bend of the head, my half closing of the eyes, that we knew so well, but it didn't work. The grin only split the dirt at the sides of your mouth and stuck. . . . When I brought him into the room your body of course had gone. . . . He liked your bed and thought he was different in it because he was a man. But one night I said let me do something, a little thing, a little trick. . . . He thought I was going to be sexually forthcoming, that I was about to take a long promised initiative. I dug about in the windowbox, where you had planted our pretty pansies, scooped, filled the bowl, and plastered his face with dirt. He resisted . . . with force. He would not let me dirty his face, or smudge it, he wouldn't let me. He suggested a wedding instead and a change of environment. (*Slight*

pause) Neither mattered. (*Pause*) He asked me once, at about that time, who had slept in that bed before him. I told him no one. No one at all.

This is the last word spoken, but after a long silence Anna walks to the door and stops there, her back towards them. Deeley begins to sob quietly. Anna switches off the lamps and lies down on one of the divans. Kate is on the other. Deeley stands, looks at both divans, goes to Anna's, goes to Kate's, sits, and then lies across her lap. He gets up, slumps into the armchair. The lights come sharply up to a maximum of brightness. As they dim the play is over.

But of course it is not over. The excited buzz of speculation which starts in the auditorium after the first public preview and goes on afterwards in conversations, in the newspapers, the weeklies, the monthlies, the books—all this is in no sense separate from the play. However hard Pinter tries to hold back from involvement with his audience, the writing, the production, and the acting cannot have developed without some consciousness of how people will react, some calculation about how much to emphasize the various suggestions that the lines, the silences, and the movements make about the relationships between the three characters.

Or are there only two? One interpretation is that Kate and Anna are two different sides of the same woman, Anna representing whatever survives of that part of the girlish self which seems to be put aside on marrying. Another is that Anna is really dead but lives on in the memories of the other two. For Harold Hobson of the *Sunday Times*, who pronounced *Old*

Times one of the finest plays of its generation, Anna, who never leaves the stage, "nevertheless is never actually on the stage at all." As Irving Wardle of *The Times* saw the play, "what it communicates intensely is the experience of three people whose lives have arrested long before, and who are searching for confirmation of the vital experiences that have faded to trivial details and emptiness in their own memories." For Ronald Bryden, then of the *Observer*, "the battleground is Kate: which of the two, Deely or Anna, has possessed more of her? The weapons, as usual, are language and sex . . . Truth has nothing to do with it." And he goes on to speculate about whether Anna really remembers a man in the bedroom with Kate. "As in *The Homecoming*," he concludes, "the final, devastating victory belongs to neither battler but to the woman battled over."

All attempts to explain the play involve an attempt to summarize something unsummarizable, and most of them enter too ingenuously into the game of finding different degrees of truthfulness in different speeches. "Yes I believed him when he said that but she wasn't telling the truth when she said that." No one in a play is telling the truth. None of the events happened in reality. But though we all know this very well, we still look for factual consistency in the fictional artifice that every play is, and Pinter is the first playwright fully to explore the theatrical potential of frustrating us.

The question of whether Anna really saw a man lying across Kate's lap is a meaningless question. What matters is the relationship between the words in which she speaks about it and the image we see at the end of the play when Deeley lies across Kate's lap. The question of whether Anna is alive or dead, an aspect of Kate, a separate person, or a set of memories in the minds of the other two is a question which deserves only a minimum of attention. It may not be wholly avoidable, but it does not need to be in the foreground of our minds; the criticism which sets out to bring it into the foreground is bad criticism. We go to the theater with our responses preconditioned by what we have heard and what we have read. *Old Times* is not a puzzle to be solved; it is an elaborate construction of words, echoing silences and images which ought to be enjoyed as such. If it makes a statement—as every play, in some sense, must—it is a statement which could not have been made by Pinter in any other way, and which remains unparaphrasable. Murder plays are usually badly written and our interest in them exhausted as soon as the mystery is solved. *Old Times* is extremely well written, and the critic can best help us to relish the writing by weaning us away from trying to solve the mysteries.

CONCLUSION

Reading Konrad Lorenz's *On Aggression*, I was struck again and again by the similarities between the animal behavior he describes and the behavior of Pinter's characters. There are so many battles for territory and battles for possession of the female. Lorenz tells us how an aquarium six feet long was not big enough for two young coral fish, scarcely an inch long. One had to live in a corner behind the bubbles of an air generator while the other patrolled the rest of the space. The main reason coral fish are colored so brightly is that this has the effect of making them fight fish who wear the same colors—not fighting to the death, but driving the rivals away so that they do not compete for the same food in the same water. The animal's readiness to fight depends partly on the distance he is from the center of the territory he "owns." Often, when one animal is chasing another away from his home territory, the fugitive, arriving on home ground, turns to attack the pursuer vigorously and unexpectedly, driving him away and pursuing; the process repeats itself until the combatants achieve a point of balance where they threaten each other without fighting. Julian Huxley has compared animal territories with air balloons pressing against each other in a glass container and expanding or contracting in accordance with the variations in internal pressure.

Most animals become vicious and more territorially greedy when they have paired. Looking at *The Homecoming* in these terms, however, Teddy has the disadvantage of being away from what is now his home and coming into the lair of a particularly aggressive family who mob together against him, as they have against Sam.

It is no accident that the motif of hunting occurs so often in Pinter's work, as it does in Beckett's. The motives for the pursuit may often remain obscure, but the panic of the quarry and the excitement of the chase are shown in animal terms. The hunt in *The Dumb Waiter* has all the more suspense for the fact that the two hunters themselves feel puzzled and hunted, afraid of what is going on outside the room. Stanley, in *The Birthday Party*, is terrified when he hears that two strangers are coming to the boarding-house and the hunt is translated into nightmare terms both in the game of blindman's buff and when the lights go out. The nightmare sequence of hunting in the dark is repeated in Pinter's screenplay for *The Servant* in the game of hide-and-seek. The master becomes like a guilty child when the adults scare him by telling him that the Bogy Man is coming for him. There are variations on the terror in the dark and on the panicky feeling that someone is after you, in Mick's pursuit of Davies with a vacuum cleaner, and in Disson's trouble with his eyes in *Tea Party*, which makes him all the more confused about the way Willy and the two women are combining to persecute him. Edward's eye trouble in *A Slight Ache* seems to hide the feeling of being threatened in some way by the matchseller, and in *A Night Out,* Sidney has had it in for Albert partly because he let the side down in the football match and partly because he is different from the others, immature, a mother's boy, quiet, not one for the girls. And in Albert, as in all the other characters, the combination of guilt with a feeling of personal inadequacy heightens the feeling of persecution. Often we get the impression of a pack of animals closing in on their prey, particularly as the girls join in the game of teasing Albert in the party scene. This is also true in *The Homecoming* when the family gang up against Teddy.

Pinter's own position, as an observer, outside things, is not unlike that of the naturalist, inspecting humanity through the glass wall of the aquarium tank. In a lecture he gave at the *Sunday Times* Student Drama Festival in 1962, he said:

> There are two silences. One when no word is spoken. The other when perhaps a torrent of language is being employed. This speech is speaking of a language locked beneath it. That is its continual reference. The speech we hear is an indication of that we don't hear. It is a necessary avoidance, a violent, sly, anguished or mocking smokescreen which keeps the other in its place. When true silence falls we are still left with echo but are nearer nakedness. One

way of looking at speech is to say it is a constant stratagem to cover nakedness.

One way of looking at Pinter's work is to say that it
is a constant stratagem to uncover nakedness. The
behavior of his characters is so seldom a reflection of
the way people normally behave and so often a reflection of the way they would like to, if they weren't
afraid to. Sometimes this behavior is a refraction of
fears and anxieties in the form of actions. Violence
occurs because animality is unleashed and, unlike the
Greeks who took a high view of human dignity and
kept the violence offstage, Pinter peers in through the
glass wall with no reverence for humanity, no belief
in our lives being mapped out by divine powers. He
has a keen eye for the cracks in the surface of normal
conversation and normal behavior. He is always on
the alert for the moments when his characters betray
what is underneath and then he simply records what
he sees and what he hears; but he does not do so in
order to evolve theories or to warn us against ourselves. His vision and his hearing are both highly
tuned instruments, invaluable in his one-man forays
into the unarticulated and irrational no-man's-land
inside the modern Everyman.

He is often accused of repeating himself, but, in his
kind of play, I do not think the charge is a damag-
ing one, except where the repetition is more of manner than of matter. In *The Homecoming* and in *Tea
Party* he was probably relying too much on the tricks
he had learned for hypnotizing an audience into rapt
attentiveness. In the screenplay for *Accident* and in
Tea Party, he manages to go over familiar territory
with unfamiliar visual images and a new speed

(again visual) in tacking from one set of images to the next. In *Landscape, Silence* and *Night* he is breaking into new ground and writing more poetically than ever before. But *Old Times* does not continue this tendency.

He once said that he dealt with his characters "at the extreme edge of their living." The later plays rely less on violence to push them into that position, but the best of them allow the characters more freedom for the violence to well up inside once they are there. While the impulses and ideas that he welcomes over the threshold of inarticulacy are still disturbing, *Old Times* is more teasing than frightening, more stylish than stylistically experimental. Success seems to have brought a security which has stilled the neurotic urgency that made the early plays so electrifying. Their triumph was to find theatrical effects that were exactly coefficient to the febrile pulsing of an inexpressible terror. The mature Pinter has mastered the demons that once possessed him. He is still a master of theatrical effects, but now they are created mainly because they are effective.

STAGE AND
BROADCAST PRODUCTIONS

London

April 1958	*The Birthday Party*, directed by Peter Wood, with Richard Pearson, at the Lyric, Hammersmith.
July 1959	*A Slight Ache*, directed by Donald McWhinnie, with Maurice Denham, on the BBC Third Programme.
January 1960	*The Room*, with Vivien Merchant, and *The Dumb Waiter*, with George Tovey and Nicholas Selby, at the Hampstead Theatre Club, transferring to the Royal Court Theatre.
March 1960	*A Night Out*, directed by Donald McWhinnie, with Barry Foster, on the BBC Third Programme.
April 1960	*The Caretaker*, directed by Donald McWhinnie, with Donald Pleasence, at the Arts Theatre.
September 1960	*Tea Party* and *The Basement*, directed by James Hammerstein, with

Donald Pleasence, Vivien Merchant, Barry Foster, and Stephanie Beacham, at the Duchess Theatre.

January 1961   *A Slight Ache*, directed by Donald McWhinnie, with Emlyn Williams, at the Arts Theatre.

May 1961   *The Collection*, directed by Joan Kemp-Welch, with John Ronane, Anthony Bate, and Griffith Jones, televised by Associated-Rediffusion.

June 1962   *The Collection*, directed by Peter Hall and Harold Pinter, with John Ronane, Kenneth Haigh, and Michael Hordern, at the Aldwych Theatre.

March 1963   *The Lover*, directed by Joan Kemp-Welch, with Vivien Merchant and Alan Badel, televised by Associated-Rediffusion.

September 1963   *The Lover*, directed by Harold Pinter, with Vivien Merchant and Scott Forbes, at the Arts Theatre.

March 1965   *Tea Party*, directed by Charles Jarrott, with Leo McKern, televised by the BBC.

June 1965   *The Homecoming*, directed by Peter Hall, with Paul Rogers and Michael Bryant, at the Aldwych Theatre.

February 1967   *The Basement*, directed by Charles Jarrott, with Derek Godfrey, Harold Pinter, and Kika Markham, televised by the BBC.

April 1968   *Landscape*, directed by Guy Vaesen, with Dame Peggy Ashcroft and Eric Porter, on the BBC Third Programme.

July 1969   *Landscape* and *Silence*, directed by Peter Hall, with Dame Peggy Ashcroft, at the Aldwych Theatre.

June 1971   *Old Times*, directed by Peter Hall, with Colin Blakely, Dorothy Tutin, and Vivien Merchant, at the Aldwych Theatre.

New York

October 1961   *The Caretaker*, directed by Donald McWhinnie, with Alan Bates, Robert Shaw, and Donald Pleasence, at the Lyceum Theatre.

November 1962   *The Dumb Waiter*, with Dana Elcar and John Becher, and *The Collection*, with Henderson Forsythe, Patricia Roe, James Ray, and James Patterson, both directed by Alan Schneider, at the Cherry Lane Theatre.

January 1964   *The Caretaker*, directed by Fred Herbert, with Norman Bowler, Donald Moffat, and Leonardo Cimino, at the Players Theatre.

January 1964   *The Lover* (with Beckett's *Play*), directed by Alan Schneider, with Hilda Brawner, Michael Lipton, and Charles Kindl, at the Cherry Lane Theatre.

December 1964   *The Room*, with Clarence Felder, Frances Sternhagen, and Ralph Drischell, and *A Slight Ache*, with Frances Sternhagen, Henderson Forsythe, and Ralph Drischell, both directed by Ward Baker, at the Writers Stage Theatre.

January 1967   *The Homecoming*, directed by Peter Hall, with Paul Rogers, Ian Holm, John Normington, and Vivian Merchant, at the Music Box.

October 1967   *The Birthday Party*, directed by Alan Schneider, with Henderson Forsythe, Ruth White, and James Patterson, at the Booth Theatre.

December 1967   *The Lover*, directed by J. Kubalek, with Jane Lahr and Lewis Rabbage, at the Cooper Square Arts Theatre.

February 1968   *The Dwarfs*, televised by National Educational Television, with Paul Benedict, F. J. Sullivan, and John Voigt.

June 1968   *The Dwarfs*, directed by Clay Stevenson, with J. Drew Lucas, at the Players Workshop.

October 1968   *Tea Party*, with David Ford, Valerie French, June Emery, and John Tillinger, and *The Basement*, with Ted van Griethuysen, James Ray, and Margo Ann Berdeshevsky, both directed by James Hammerstein, at the Eastside Playhouse.

April 1970   *Landscape*, with Robert Symonds and Mildred Natwick, and *Silence*, with Barbara Tarbuck, Robert Symonds, and James Patterson, both directed by Peter Gill, at the Forum Theater, Lincoln Center.

February 1971   *Birthday Party*, directed by Jules Irving, with Ray Fry, Betty Field, and Robert Phalen, at the Forum Theater, Lincoln Center.

May 1971   *The Homecoming*, directed by Jerry Adler, with Eric Berry, Tony Tan-

<table>
<tr><td></td><td>ner, Norman Barrs, and Janice Rule, at the Bijou Theatre.</td></tr>
<tr><td>November 1971</td><td>A Night Out, with Elice Higgenbotham, Eve Dmytryk, and William Snickowski, at the Park Avenue Community Theatre.</td></tr>
<tr><td>November 1971</td><td>Old Times, directed by Peter Hall, with Robert Shaw, Rosemary Harris, and Mary Ure, at the Billy Rose Theater.</td></tr>
<tr><td>April 1973</td><td>Monologue, directed by Christopher Morahan, with Henry Woolf, televised by the BBC.</td></tr>
</table>

BIBLIOGRAPHY

WORKS BY PINTER

The Birthday Party, and The Room: Two Plays. New York: Grove Press, 1961.

The Caretaker, and The Dumb Waiter. New York: Grove Press, 1961.

Three Plays. New York: Grove Press, 1962. (Includes *A Slight Ache, The Collection,* and *The Dwarfs.*)

The Collection and The Lover. London: Methuen, 1964.

The Homecoming. New York: Grove Press, 1966.

The Lover. Tea Party. The Basement. New York: Grove Press, 1967.

A Night Out. Night School. Revue Sketch. New York: Grove Press, 1968.

Landscape and Silence. New York: Grove Press, 1970.

Old Times. New York: Grove Press, 1972.

In Great Britain all the plays are published by Methuen & Co. Ltd. *Monologue* was published by Covent Garden Press, 1973.

WORKS ABOUT PINTER

Burkman, Kartherine H. *The Dramatic World of Harold Pinter: Its Basis in Ritual.* Columbus: Ohio State University Press, 1971.

Dias, Earl J. "The Enigmatic World of Harold Pinter." *Drama Critique* 11, no. 3 (fall 1968):119–48.

Esslin, Martin. *The People Wound: The Work of Harold Pinter.* Garden City, N.Y.: Doubleday, 1970.

Gordon, Lois G. "Pigeonholing Pinter: A Bibliography." *Theatre Document* 1, no. 1 (fall 1968): 3–20.

Gussow, Mel. "A Conversation [Pause] with Harold Pinter." *New York Times Magazine*, 5 December 1971.

Hollis, James R. *Harold Pinter: The Poetics of Silence.* Carbondale: Southern Illinois University Press, 1970.

Lahr, John, ed. *A Casebook on Harold Pinter's "The Homecoming."* New York: Grove Press, 1971.

Orley, Ray. "Pinter and Menace." *Drama Critique* 11, no. 3 (fall 1968).

Schroll, Herman T. *Harold Pinter: A Study of His Reputation (1958–1969) and a Checklist.* Metuchen, N.J.: Scarecrow Press, 1971.

Trussler, Simon. *The Plays of Harold Pinter.* London: Gollancz, 1973.

INDEX

The Nyack Library
845-358-3370